Theatre in Towns

Theatre in Towns offers a contemporary perspective on the role of theatre in the cultural life of towns in England. Exploring volunteer-led, professional and community theatres, this book investigates the rich and diverse ways that theatres in towns serve their locality, negotiate their civic role, participate in networks of mutual aid and exchange, and connect audiences beyond their geographical borders.

With a geographical focus on post-industrial, seaside, commuter and market towns in England, the book opens questions about how theatre shapes the narratives of town life, and how localism, networks and partnerships across and between towns contribute to living sustainably. Each chapter is critically and historically informed, drawing on original research in towns, including visits to performances and many conversations with townspeople, from theatre-makers, performers, set-builders, front-of-house volunteers, to audience members and civic leaders. *Theatre in Towns* asks urgent questions about how the relationships between towns and theatres can be redefined in new and equitable ways in the future.

Theatre in Towns brings new research to scholars and students of theatre studies, cultural geography, cultural and social policy and political sociology. It will also interest artists, policy-makers and researchers wanting to develop their own and others' understanding of the value of active theatre cultures in towns.

Helen Nicholson is Professor of Theatre and Performance at Royal Holloway, University of London, UK. Her research addresses theatre in community settings, often focusing on theatre in places that are overlooked. She has published widely on applied theatre, theatre education, amateur theatre and participatory arts.

Jenny Hughes is Professor of Drama at the University of Manchester, UK. Her research engages with the intersections of socially-engaged performance, economic justice and social change agendas, and activist art. She has published on theatre and performance in relation to socio-economic inequality, protest events, histories of welfare and political emergency.

Gemma Edwards is a Leverhulme Early Career Fellow at the University of Manchester, UK. Her work focuses on place, politics, and performance, particularly in non-metropolitan contexts. She has published on rurality in contemporary theatre, and her next project explores race, class, and English nationhood from 1945 to the present.

Cara Gray was a postdoctoral researcher on the *Civic Theatres: A Place for Towns* project, at Royal Holloway, University of London, UK. She is an interdisciplinary researcher whose work sits across theatre and performance and cultural geography. Past research has explored the cultural geographies of amateur creativity: publishing on the spaces, materialities, and creative processes of backstage theatre-makers, specifically set-builders.

Theatre in Towns

Helen Nicholson, Jenny Hughes,
Gemma Edwards, and Cara Gray

Routledge
Taylor & Francis Group
LONDON AND NEW YORK

First published 2023
by Routledge
4 Park Square, Milton Park, Abingdon, Oxon OX14 4RN

and by Routledge
605 Third Avenue, New York, NY 10158

Routledge is an imprint of the Taylor & Francis Group, an informa business

© 2023 Helen Nicholson, Jenny Hughes, Gemma Edwards, and Cara Gray

The right of Helen Nicholson, Jenny Hughes, Gemma Edwards, and Cara Gray to be identified as authors of this work has been asserted in accordance with sections 77 and 78 of the Copyright, Designs and Patents Act 1988.

The Open Access version of this book, available at www.taylorfrancis.com, has been made available under a Creative Commons Attribution-Non Commercial-No Derivatives 4.0 license.

Trademark notice: Product or corporate names may be trademarks or registered trademarks, and are used only for identification and explanation without intent to infringe.

British Library Cataloguing-in-Publication Data
A catalogue record for this book is available from the British Library

Library of Congress Cataloging-in-Publication Data
Names: Nicholson, Helen, 1958- author. | Hughes, Jenny, 1971- author. | Edwards, Gemma, author. | Gray, Cara, author.
Title: Theatre in towns/Helen Nicholson, Jenny Hughes, Gemma Edwards and Cara Gray.
Description: Abingdon, Oxon; New York, NY: Routledge, 2023. | Includes bibliographical references and index.
Identifiers: LCCN 2022043928 (print) | LCCN 2022043929 (ebook) | ISBN 9781032311050 (hardback) | ISBN 9781032444352 (paperback) | ISBN 9781003308058 (ebook)
Subjects: LCSH: Theater and society–England. | Cities and towns–England.
Classification: LCC PN2049 .N56 2023 (print) | LCC PN2049 (ebook) | DDC 792.0942–dc23/eng/20220926
LC record available at https://lccn.loc.gov/2022043928
LC ebook record available at https://lccn.loc.gov/2022043929

ISBN: 978-1-032-31105-0 (hbk)
ISBN: 978-1-032-44435-2 (pbk)
ISBN: 978-1-003-30805-8 (ebk)

DOI: 10.4324/9781003308058

Typeset in Times New Roman
by KnowledgeWorks Global Ltd.

Contents

List of Figures	vi
Acknowledgements	vii
1 **Theatres in Towns: Places of Hope and Experiment** JENNY HUGHES AND HELEN NICHOLSON	1
2 **Local Theatres: Cultures of Participation** HELEN NICHOLSON	12
3 **Making a Civic Spectacle: Towns for Rent** JENNY HUGHES	41
4 **Volunteer-Led Theatres: Meshworks of a Coastal Town** CARA GRAY	66
5 **Made to Connect: Theatrical Exchange between Town and City** GEMMA EDWARDS	93
6 **Hopeful Futures: Theatres in Towns** GEMMA EDWARDS AND CARA GRAY	116
Index	127

Figures

2.1	*I am a bird*, Artist, Marie Klimis	20
2.2	Love Slough – *The Dance WE Made* by Casson & Friends	25
2.3	Wallingford Corn Exchange on the market square	27
2.4	Wallingford's Mayor, Marcus Harris, opening Bunkfest 2022	29
2.5	Sign on Corn Exchange inviting new people to volunteer, September 2022	35
3.1	The cast at The Old Courts. From left to right – Yasmin Goulden, Zha Olu, Darren Pritchard, Jamie Lee, Shaun Fallows, Stuart Bowden, Sarah Hardman, Alice Mae Fairhurst	55
3.2	Shaun Fallows – Rent Party, *Wigan*	58
4.1	Hastings Pier	68
4.2	Stables Theatre, Hastings	77
4.3	Stables Theatre backstage crew	80
5.1	Spinners Mill, Leigh	96

Acknowledgements

Theatre in Towns arose from a wider research project, *Civic Theatres: A Place for Towns*, funded by the Arts and Humanities Research Council [grant number AH/T012609/1]. We are grateful to the AHRC and to all our partners in this research project, the Royal Exchange Theatre, The Little Theatre Guild, and The National Theatre, and to the collaborating organisation, Tribe Arts, all of whom contributed to the research with insight and generosity. We have also valued discussions with academics during the research, particularly those who contributed to events and symposia. Our research was enriched by many theatre-makers and townspeople across the country who shared their thoughts, ideas, stories, and experiences in numerous on-line events, focus groups, interviews, rehearsals, and performances. We are especially indebted to the theatres and cultural organisations which served as case studies in this book including Breaking Barriers, Rochdale; Farnham Maltings; Home Slough; Letchworth Settlement Players; The Old Courts, Wigan; Spinners Mill, Leigh; The Corn Exchange, Wallingford; Stables Theatre, Hastings. We have appreciated the warm welcome and generosity of spirit we encountered in every town we visited, and we thank everyone for sharing their experiences and vision for theatres in towns.

1 Theatres in Towns
Places of Hope and Experiment

Jenny Hughes and Helen Nicholson

While we were researching theatre in towns for this book, a performance was taking place across Europe. Little Amal, a giant child-refugee puppet, began a walk from Gazientep in Turkey, close to the Syrian border, a city that had become home to half a million refugees during the ten-year-long war. Little Amal travelled more than 8000 kilometres between June and November 2021, visiting over 70 towns, villages and cities, before ending her journey in Manchester in the UK. *The Walk* was co-produced by Good Chance Theatre, a company founded as a creative response to the Calais refugee camp in 2015, in partnership with Handspring Puppet Company. Her walk created spontaneous moments of encounter across the streets, squares, neighbourhoods, and civic and cultural institutions of Europe, with more than 875,000 people gathering to watch, accompany or stage choreographed acts of welcome. Evoking strong emotional responses everywhere she walked, the performance materialised a chain reaction of support and care.

We met Little Amal twice on her walk. First, at the National Theatre in London, and then in Wigan, a town close to Manchester. On a sunny afternoon in London, she was greeted by members of the Public Acts company, the National Theatre's programme of new works created in partnership with theatres and communities across the UK. Lifting candles above their heads, the cast of the inaugural Public Acts production, *Pericles*, sang to Little Amal from the theatre's balconies. *I am my own way home* (composer Jim Fortune, lyricist Chris Bush) is a haunting song that captures the joy of finding a home after the pain of loss and abandonment. A few weeks later, on a cold and rainy day in Wigan, we followed Little Amal's walk through the Wigan Pier quarter, where she met the Mayor of Greater Manchester, Andy Burnham, danced with the youth group, WigLe Dance, before heading to a conference centre where local groups presented her with

DOI: 10.4324/9781003308058-1

a quilt and read her stories. Along the way she enjoyed performances by a community choir and Wigan Youth Brass Band, and listened to a poem performed by local poet Louise Fazackerley, who wore an elaborate dress made of recycled packaging from Wigan family business, Uncle Joe's mint balls.

'Amal', the Arabic word for hope, is an appropriate name for a performance designed to transform negative narratives associated with the 'refugee crisis' into small acts of welcome, rooted in the affective and social relationships of places and communities. Little Amal was a response to adversity characterised by hopeful forms of collective and creative action, and this resonates with the research that led to this book. Our research in towns across England took place at a significant moment of time. Starting in 2020 when theatres were closed due to the global Covid-19 pandemic and concluding in 2022 when most restrictions had been lifted, it coincided with a period of intense challenge for towns, leading many theatres and cultural organisations to pause and reassess their priorities. On a national scale, health and related inequalities within and between towns and cities became sharply visible, with commentators powerfully pointing out how these are embedded in longer histories of poverty, racism, and colonialism (Bump et al, 2021). Keeping Little Amal in mind, in this opening chapter we draw on hope as a metaphor to explore the affective qualities, material practices, and cultural value of theatres in towns through and beyond such challenging times. Rebecca Solnit's poetic essay, *Hope in the Dark* (2016), argues that hope is intimately related to an impetus to act, particularly in places and times of uncertainty:

> Hope locates itself in the premises that we don't know what will happen and that in the spaciousness of uncertainty is room to act … Hope is an embrace of the unknown and the unknowable, an alternative to the certainty of both optimists and pessimists.
> (Solnit, 2016, p. xii)

Throughout our research we – a research team of four – found that the work of theatres in towns balanced responses to local, regional, and global challenges with an openness to re-imagining and re-making what life might become. In this chapter, we present the aims and context of the research and introduce the chapters that follow. As we lay out the terrain of the book, we unfold an idea of theatre as a hopeful, collective, and practical form of action that generates experiences, onstage and off-stage, in ways that cannot be described neatly as optimistic or pessimistic, or aligned with politically Left or Right perspectives. Instead, mindful of what Solnit calls 'an untold history of people power' which intersects with hope,[1] we centre the imagination, creativity, and pragmatism expressed by many of the people we encountered in theatres in towns as we researched this book.

Why theatres in towns?

Our starting point is that towns are distinct places and demand perspectives that extend beyond rural or city-focused viewpoints. But towns are notoriously difficult to define, particularly in a UK context where distinctions between towns, cities, and villages can only be understood with reference to complex and contingent layers of history. Unlike many other parts of the world where cities are classified by size and density of population, in the UK, the ceremonial title of city, a title that distinguishes cities from towns, is still conferred by Royal decree. For many rural communities, towns serve as local centres of commerce, entertainment, and civic amenities, and although the medieval practice of granting royal charters to European market towns died out long ago, the historic status of many towns remains widely celebrated as a mark of civic pride. Despite the growth of cities in recent global history, the Office for National Statistics reports that – in 2017 – over half the population of England and Wales (56%) were living in towns. The same report highlights the diversity of towns, with the definition of a town extending from small towns of 5000–20,000 to large towns of up to 225,000 people (ONS, 2019). The Centre for Towns, a non-partisan organisation founded in 2017 to build evidence-based research about UK towns, argued that towns deserve far more attention from policy-makers and researchers than they have received to date. Categorising towns by size of population (small, medium, and large) as well as by type (market, seaside, post-industrial, university, commuter, and new towns), the Centre for Towns makes the case that towns have specific qualities such as cultural, social, and economic hubs. In their Launch Briefing, Wigan MP Lisa Nandy stated:

> For far too long towns have been ignored, patronised and labelled 'left behind' allowing the assets, skills and aspirations within them to go untapped and unrealised. Those assets are alive and well in towns like Wigan, where protecting the environment and good public services are a priority, and skills, tightly knit communities and a strong sense of shared history and identity are plentiful. With the right thinking, they hold the clue to a better future.
> (Nandy, 2017, p. 1)

Despite this argument for a new focus on towns, city status remains an aspiration for many large towns in the UK, attracted by the promise of increased economic productivity and prosperity associated with cities, despite the socioeconomic inequalities that this has also produced. As Lisa Nandy infers, cities have dominated the political agenda, shaping collective understandings of what 'good' or productive economies might look like, including creative economies. This is also the case in the cultural sector, with the term 'creative city', introduced by Charles Landry in the 1990s and popularised by Richard Florida, allying the creative industries firmly to the kind of entrepreneurship and privatisation of urban space associated with neoliberalism and gentrification of the city (Mould, 2018, p. 155).

Theatre in Towns is in part motivated by a positive interest in how towns might avoid the inequalities associated with an unregulated, market-led approach to theatre and performance which many have observed in city cultures (Harvie 2013, pp. 133–134). Our discipline is dominated by analyses of performance that takes place in cities, with substantial studies addressing the performance culture of cities explicitly (McKinnie, 2007; Harvie, 2009; Whybrow, 2010), but there is surprisingly little research that engages directly with theatres in towns. There are exceptions: important historical research on regional theatre includes theatres in towns (Turnbull, 2009; Dorney and Merkin, 2010; Cochrane, 2011), and towns feature in recent studies of amateur theatre as well as socially engaged theatre (Nicholson, Holdsworth and Milling, 2018; Dunn and Hughes, 2019; Gray, 2020). There is also a significant strand of research addressing theatre in rural environments (Robinson, 2016; Edwards, 2020). By situating our research firmly in English towns, we aim to decentre theatre and performance studies by looking at contemporary theatre from another point of view. In this book we locate theatre in towns within the broader systems of cultural value and cultural economies in which they operate and, by situating our research in England, we have attempted to avoid generalisations about other UK nations. The cultural ecosystems in England's towns tend to be organically networked, with a mixture of volunteers, professional theatre-makers, and community partners finding ways to work together to create sustainable projects and initiatives. It is important to note that productive collaborations between different parts of the cultural sector, local people, public funders, and business communities have a long and radical history in towns. Labour MP Jennie Lee's manifesto for the arts in 1965 advocated systems of funding in which local arts enthusiasts – both amateur and professional – worked with local businesses and local authorities to finance arts projects and events 'that few local authorities by themselves could afford' (Lee, 1965, p. 11).

Today's funding landscape is even more challenging than in the 1960s. In our research we encountered theatres in towns that are at risk and where their cultural assets have either closed or are suffering from long-term neglect or threat of closure. Theatres and cultural organisations that rely on local authority funding were particularly vulnerable in the context of economic austerity, the policy adopted by successive Conservative governments following the financial crash in 2007–2008. Between 2010 and 2018 central government grants to local government reduced by 49.1% and the impact on local authority arts funding was 'deleterious' but regionally uneven, with decision-making varying in response to localised priorities (Rex and Campbell, 2022, p. 41). The pandemic further amplified existing socioeconomic inequalities, adding to long-term pressures on resources for health and social care services and, with rising living costs, this context continues to mean that some local authorities find it hard to justify spending their money on the arts. The cost-of-living crisis follows a long period of political turmoil in the UK, associated with the close referendum vote to leave the European Union in 2016 ('Brexit'). Geographer Philip McCann has argued persuasively that the leave vote in towns and villages revealed a 'geography of discontent' fuelled by a sense that the needs of people and places outside of major cities had not been addressed by the political mainstream (McCann, 2020). This period of political turmoil has led to a raft of government-led and influenced initiatives that, during the period of our research, transformed the funding landscape for towns in England. The slogan 'levelling up' has been used to describe a major government-led policy initiative that aims to address longstanding inequalities of opportunity across the UK (which has the larger regional differences on multiple economic measures than countries with similar economies). While recognising the potential of such a move, political scientists Will Jennings and colleagues have argued persuasively that 'levelling up' is an example of government by 'political spectacle' designed to capture votes, and that its internal contradictions 'may only reinforce socioeconomic divides between major cities and outlying towns' (Jennings, McKay and Stoker, 2021, p. 307).

Nonetheless, public subsidy for the arts has followed this political trend, leading to what an Arts Council England report on creative high streets has called 'unprecedented' levels of investment for cultural infrastructure (Lewis, Lili and Cringle, 2022, p. 10). While this may be overstating the case, during our research we encountered many theatres and performance venues in towns that were taking advantage of new opportunities for funding from schemes connected to public bodies such as Arts Council England and Historic England, the various Towns Funds associated with government policies, as well as finding philanthropic support from charities and foundations. Although cultural resources in some towns remain stretched and under threat, we also visited beautifully equipped theatres that were once derelict civic or commercial buildings. Many had been carefully restored by local enthusiasts working in partnership with local authorities and businesses in ways that Jennie Lee would recognise, and now serving as creative and cultural centres for their town. Investing time and resources in a town's theatre can create feelings of ownership and open spaces for community programming and local events in ways that would be difficult to imagine in most London theatres. As part of this, dispersed modes of coproduction, new partnerships, commissioning, and touring arrangements have strengthened existing models of collaboration.

Though it is possible to read approaches to sustaining theatres in towns as encouraging the kind of self-help and self-entrepreneurship favoured by the political Right, the cultural life in towns is more nuanced and complex than this reading would imply. It is of course essential to continue to make a case for public subsidy for the arts to generate a rich and dynamic cultural life, particularly for people without regular access to the arts. Well-targeted public funding is also needed to support local artists who wish to develop satisfying creative careers without having to move to the nearest city. We would also argue that alternative socio-economic structures that include mutual aid and circular and gift economies, when supported by intersectional working practices, contribute to fostering resilience in several ways. First, an emphasis on self-generated activity, supported by professional, amateur, and voluntary partnerships, are distinct and historic features of the cultural life of towns. Second, the scale of towns and their distinctive cultural ecologies means that there is potential for local artists and communities to come together in multiple settings, including theatre. Regular cultural encounters, sharing spaces, and building sociability and friendship generate the kind of hopefulness that, Solnit suggests, leads people to keep pursuing possibilities for change (Solnit, 2016, p. 141). Third, theatres are places of experiment that offer productive spaces in which local artists and communities can prefigure imaginative responses to emergent challenges. Sociologist Bruno Latour offered a description of such challenges as created by globalisation, an explosion of inequalities and climate crisis, which should be understood as 'symptoms of a single historical situation'. Importantly, he identifies this as a problem of scale and – evoking the imaginary landscape forged by Little Amal in her journey across a continent – he comments 'We must face up to what is literally a problem of dimension, scale, and lodging ... We are all overwhelmed twice over: by what is too big, and by what is too small' (Latour, 2018, p. 16).

Inside this doubly weighted space, theatres in towns offer places for experimentation and for lodging. They are tightly bound up with individual and collective identity, biography, and belonging, providing what Latour calls 'inhabitable land' (Latour, p. 16) for negotiating, experimenting, and projecting a way through global challenges that are felt and experienced locally. Theatres in towns we visited are not tied to ideas of experiment that break with the past, valorise the new, or seek to move on from tradition. Rather, they embrace custom and innovation and capture a sense of experimentation that comes from many small acts of creation over time, working in concert with existing forms, relationships, and places, to create spaces of hope, sustainability, and resilience. Terms such as circular, networked, small-scale, inclusive and diverse, iterative, partial, hybrid, improvised, stop and start, DIY, messy, practical and pragmatic describe the registers of experiment that we witnessed during this research. Often these experiments were ends in themselves, creating their own benefits – providing a social network to combat isolation or a symbol of renewal for a neighbourhood, for example. But they also had more sustained outcomes – a new venue for townspeople, a new partnership supporting a range of initiatives, or successful community events that triggered additional investment.

Researching theatre in towns: Our approach

Our research aimed to capture theatre activity in English towns at a historical juncture where established models of cultural practice were realigning in response to new challenges and opportunities. We were interested in understanding the commonalities that emerged when contemporary theatre and performance practices in towns were examined alongside each other as well as within their specific geocultural and historical localities. We were influenced in our choice of towns for detailed case studies by the Centre for Towns' classification of towns in terms of size and type and, in the chapters that follow, we reflect on theatre that takes place in coastal towns, market towns, new towns, commuter towns, and post-industrial towns. We anticipate that the issues we encountered in towns across England will have resonance in towns across the UK as well as in similar urban contexts beyond our shores.

Four key thematic areas emerged from our research, all of which have international relevance: localism and cultural participation; civic cultures and regeneration; volunteerism and the gift economy; and cultural exchange and partnerships. These four themes provide the conceptual framework for the book, and although they cut across all our research, they are analysed in depth in separate chapters, using particular towns as case studies. Chapter 2, written by Helen Nicholson, examines what it means to participate in local theatres. Localism is associated with an idealised vision of connected, place-based communities and local decision-making, but there is also a risk that localism becomes associated with parochialism and resistance to change. Four towns in the South East region – Farnham, Chesham, Slough, and Wallingford – illustrate how local theatres are challenging this perception. Questions of civic life run throughout our research on towns, and in Chapter 3, Jenny Hughes focuses on the relationship between theatre and civic culture in towns, analysing the ways in which civic ideals are reproduced and reinvented by arts activity, and examining a theatrical experiment in the town of Wigan. Many theatres we visited are run by enthusiasts who voluntarily give up their time and Cara Gray explores this in Chapter 4, where she reflects on her research in Hastings and other coastal towns to investigate how resident volunteers and professional and amateur theatre-makers contribute to cultures of care and gift economies in towns. One of the central themes of our research relates to the ways that cultural exchanges between community groups and theatres can sustain theatrical activity in towns. Gemma Edwards' analysis of Leigh in Greater Manchester demonstrates how major theatres and people engaged in a variety of cultural ventures in towns can work together. The book concludes by revisiting the themes of hope opened in this first chapter, offering examples of towns that have gifted cities with new ways of living, working, and playing that remain resonant today.

Taken as a whole, the book reflects on a range of creative practices. Some artistic repertoires evolve when theatre-makers in towns and cities work in partnership, and others are inspired by townspeople and local artists. Building-based theatres and cultural venues are catalysts for a variety of performance practices, frequently attracting participants and audiences in ways that, as the Future Arts Centres campaign advocates, erodes divisions between art forms.[2] In Chapter 2 Helen Nicholson describes a range of local initiatives in the South East that include amateur repertoires familiar to local performers, approaches to community programming, and models of co-production with non-theatrical venues that re-invent the popular theatres of the 1970s advocated by John McGrath. Other projects were based on partnerships between arts venues in towns and cities – the model of co-production that led to *Rent Party*, discussed by Jenny Hughes in Chapter 3, was conceived by town and city-based producers and artists working together, finding distinct forms of expression and meaning in each site of co-production, including, as explored in this chapter, with audiences in the town of Wigan. In Chapter 5, Cara Gray encountered a hybrid model of theatre-making in the seaside town of Hastings, where professional playwrights and local artists have found a new place to experiment in their volunteer-run theatre, part of the Little Theatre Guild network. As Gemma Edwards writes in Chapter 5, city theatres are developing new models of exchange with cultural organisations in the regions in ways that seek to engage with the distinct cultural heritage of a place, in this case the town of Leigh. Our research repeatedly drew attention to the mixed economy of theatre in towns, where intersections between different theatre sectors, and between theatre and other performance forms, including live comedy and live art and music, are well-trodden and well-established.

This book shows how theatres can be profoundly important to a town's cultural and social ecology – bringing people together for enjoyment and social occasions and creating a sense of belonging, identity, and memory. This was powerfully illustrated by the walk of Little Amal across Europe, and the crowds that gathered to witness her story. So much of this book is inspired by the sense of optimism we witnessed during our research, and it seems fitting to conclude by returning to a metaphor of hope, with Solnit's words: 'Changing the story isn't enough in itself, but it has been foundational to real changes. Making an injury visible and public is often the first stage to remedying it, and political change often follows culture' (Solnit, 2016, p. xiv).

Notes

1. 'An untold history of people power' was the sub-heading of the first edition of Solnit's essay on hope, published in 2004.
2. This egalitarian attitude is a historical feature of the art centre movement in the UK, and has been given new impetus by the recent Future Arts Centres campaign. For more information: https://futureartscentres.org.uk/ [Accessed 10 August 2022]

References

Bump, J, Baum, F, Sakornsin, M, Yates, R and Hofman, K. (2021). 'Political Economy of Covid-19: Extractive, Regressive, Competitive', *The BMJ*, 372, p. n73.

Cochrane, C. (2011). *Twentieth Century British Theatre: Industry, Art and Empire*. Cambridge: Cambridge University Press.

Dorney, K. and Merkin, R. (eds.) (2010). *The Glory of the Garden: English Regional Theatre and the Arts Council 1984–2009*. Newcastle upon Tyne: Cambridge Scholars.

Dunn, B. and Hughes, J. (2019). 'The Theatre Dividend' in Mullen, M. (eds.), *Applied Theatre: Economies*. London & New York: Methuen.

Edwards, G. (2020). 'Small Stories, Local Places: A Place-Oriented Approach to Rural Crises', *Journal of Contemporary Drama in English*, 8(1), pp. 64–82.

Gray, C. (2020). 'The Repairer and the Ad Hocist: Understanding the 'ongoingness' of the Amateur Theatre maker's Craft', *Performance Research*, 25(1), pp. 88–95.

Harvie, J. (2009). *Theatre & the City*. Basingstoke: Palgrave Macmillan.

Harvie, J. (2013). *Fair Play: Art, Performance and Neoliberalism*. Basingstoke: Palgrave Macmillan.

Jennings, W, McKay, L and Stoker, G. (2021). 'The Politics of Levelling Up', *The Political Quarterly*, 92(2), pp. 302–311.

Latour, B. (2018). *Down to Earth: Politics in the New Climatic Regime*. Cambridge: Polity Press.

Lee, J. (1965). *A Policy for the Arts: The First Steps*. London: HMSO.

Lewis, H, Lili, L and Cringle, B. (2022). Creative High Streets. PRD, Arts Council England & South East Local Enterprise Partnerships. Available at: https://www.artscouncil.org.uk/sites/default/files/download-file/We%20Made%20That_231_SELEP%20Creative%20high%20streets_220131.pdf (Accessed 24 June 2022).

McCann, P. (2020). 'Perceptions of Regional Inequality and the Geography of Discontent: Insights from the UK', *Regional Studies*, 54(2), pp. 256–267.

McKinnie, M. (2007). *City Stages: Theatre and Urban Space in a Global City*. Toronto: University of Toronto Press.

Mould, O. (2018). *Against Creativity*. London & New York: Verso.

Nandy, L. (2017). Centre for Towns Launch Briefing. Available at: www.centrefortowns.org (Accessed 17 December 2021).

Nicholson, H, Holdsworth, N and Milling, J. (2018). *The Ecologies of Amateur Theatre*. London: Palgrave Macmillan.

Office for National Statistics (ONS). (2019). Understanding towns in England and Wales. Available at: https://www.ons.gov.uk/peoplepopulationandcommunity/populationandmigration/populationestimates/articles/understandingtownsinenglandandwales/anintroduction (Accessed 10 August 2022).

Rex, B and Campbell, P. (2022). 'The Impact of Austerity Measures on Local Government Funding for Culture in England', *Cultural Trends*, 31(1), pp. 23–46.

Robinson, J. (2016). *Theatre and the Rural*. Basingstoke: Palgrave Macmillan.
Solnit, R. (2016). *Hope in the Dark: Untold Histories, Wild Possibilities*. Edinburgh: Canongate.
Turnbull, O. (2009). *Bringing Down the House: The Crisis in Britain's Regional Theatres*. Bristol, UK and Chicago, USA: Intellect.
Whybrow, N. (eds.). (2010). *Performance and the Contemporary City: An Interdisciplinary Reader*. Basingstoke: Palgrave Macmillan.

2 Local Theatres
Cultures of Participation
Helen Nicholson

Places tell stories. Stories are inscribed in the built environment, memorialised in public spaces, and entangled in layers of memory. Local stories are mythologised, landmarks become haunted, and places are marked by stories that are told and retold as half-remembered recollections. When the COVID pandemic began in 2020 and travel was restricted, many people explored their local area on foot, following unfamiliar paths in places they thought they knew well. The experience of regular walking added to their repertoire of stories and re-shaped their sense of place. This physical act of walking, the anthropologist Tim Ingold suggests, enables pedestrians to sense the environment in their bodies, their habitual movements working with the environment to make what he calls 'a tangled mesh of personalised trails' (Ingold, 2011, p. 47). Successive generations of 'personalised trails' contribute to towns' histories, generating place-based identities by connecting local knowledge with autobiographical experience. Stories construct what it means to be local, creating feelings of belonging that are felt particularly keenly by long-standing residents.

Theatres in towns are integral to the localised production of cultural life, connecting trails with stories as Ingold describes. Frequently described as 'local theatres', they can forge close relationships with townspeople and shape the annual rhythm of town life. In turn, many theatres incentivise loyalty with discounted tickets for multiple bookings, membership schemes and, in commercial theatres, corporate packages for local businesses with the promise of increased brand recognition and access to visiting West End stars. Theatre audiences bring much-needed revenue to local economies but, as Ben Walmsley suggests, measuring the arts only according to their economic value misses other important qualities. He calls for wider recognition of

DOI: 10.4324/9781003308058-2

the cultural value of the arts within an expanded field of audience research:

> This culture shift will require a fundamental reconceptualisation of value, from the traditional dominance of quantifiable metrics such as ticket price and yield towards a broader focus on aesthetic and social (i.e. cultural) value.
> (Walmsley, 2019, p. 101)

This chapter takes up Walmsley's challenge by reflecting on the cultural value of theatres in towns, and their contribution to local life. It starts with the premise that the scale and distinctiveness of towns offer opportunities for deeper and more sustained relationships between theatres and local audiences than is possible in many cities. David Gauntlett's slogan 'making is connecting' (Gauntlett, 2011) is particularly apposite for theatres in towns; local theatres benefit from the craft, creativity, and sociability of local people, whether they are amateur theatre-makers, professional artists, volunteers, or community participants. Theatre buildings are rich in memory, and performances in town squares, high streets, and other public spaces affect the ways in which towns are lived, felt, and perceived.

Yet the 'local' and localism carries multiple meanings, and living locally is not only experienced differently by townspeople, local life is also defined by the distinctive histories and identities of each town. On the one hand, the local is associated with an environmental ideal, a vision of sustainability, where independent shops, mutual aid, economies of care, and cultural activities are integral to community wellbeing. On the other, localism can make towns appear insular, complacent, inhospitable, and resistant to change. Architects and urban theorists Simin Davoudi and Ali Madanipour describe this contradiction in political terms:

> Localism is seen as: a re-ordering and liberalisation of political spaces, a site of empowerment, a locus of knowledge generation, a framework for social integration and community-building, a localisation of economic activities and a site of resistance and environmental activism. The motivations for localism range from communitarian intents to liberal and libertarian agendas and are riddled with tensions between progressive and regressive potentials.
> (Davoudi and Madanipour, 2015, p. 1)

The towns represented in this chapter actively negotiate this paradox in practice. Each town discussed is different in character and access to resources, and all are in South East England, a region widely considered affluent. Yet economic prosperity is not evenly distributed across the region, and in every town I visited (Farnham, Surrey; Chesham and High Wycombe, Buckinghamshire; Slough in Berkshire; Wallingford, Oxfordshire) there is considerable deprivation alongside more well-off areas. Each town navigates contemporary challenges, including post-industrialism, changing patterns of work, housing and commuting, and the effects of climate change. Towns are particularly good places to encourage localised resilience, and strengthening local economies is widely regarded as a route to sustainable living. Rob Hopkins, co-founder of the Transition Network, invokes eco-localism as a practical approach to a low carbon economy, with a local food, local trading, and renewable energy united under the strapline 'local action can change the world' (Hopkins, 2013, p. 11).

So what does it mean to be a local theatre? As sites where stories of place and identity are constructed and told, theatres are complexly entangled in the political ambiguities surrounding localism. The insights of social anthropologist Arjun Appadurai are illuminating. Drawing on the work of Raymond Williams, he describes locality as a 'structure of feeling' that is produced and reproduced through imagination, embodiment, story, and sociality (Appadurai, 2008, pp. 178–180). Producing neighbourhoods, by contrast, involves imposing social order, a process he regards as 'inherently colonising' (Appadurai, 2008, p. 183). Creating equitable communities – in theatres and elsewhere – depends on narratives of place that are open and inclusive. Conversely, as Madanipour and Davoudi argue, stories of place that promote homogeneous local identities risk reproducing inequalities:

> The stable narrative about the identity of a place may reflect existing power-relations in that locality. Diversity of experience and the material conditions of a locality, therefore, may be narrowed down in the construction of an overarching narrative into which the locality is introduced.
> (Madanipour and Davoudi, 2015, p. 23)

This has implications for theatre, as theatre historian Joseph Roach contends: 'a fixed and unified culture exists only as a convenient but dangerous fiction' (Roach, 1996, p. 5). Roach's warnings have become increasingly prescient, and challenges to homogenous cultural histories have been dangerously weaponised. When Corinne Fowler addressed how colonialism and the slave trade remained imprinted on the countryside, and Sathnam Sanghera confronted how racism in Britain is perpetuated by unresolved relationships with its imperial past (Sanghera, 2021), they both received serious abuse. As Fowler observes, 'Repressed histories only *appear* contentious because they are unfamiliar' (Fowler, 2020, p. 30, italics original).

The paradox that surrounds localism – as a force of progressive and regressive politics – means that it has found favour across the political spectrum. In England, localism's political porosity is evident in the Localism Act in 2011, where the Conservative and Liberal Democrat Coalition government found common ground in localism as a route to decentralising the State's powers. Writing in 2014, geographers Andrew Williams, Mark Goodwin, and Paul Cloke summarised this version of localism as:

> the implicit ideals of philanthropy, self-help, and volunteerism through the devolution of power from the state to local communities [which] continue to be rolled out in a number of policy initiatives, not least the Localism Act 2011.
> (Andrews, Godwin, and Cloke, 2014, p. 2298)

The Localism Act (2011) introduced Neighbourhood Development Plans to encourage community voice in planning decisions, strengthened in 2017 by the Neighbourhood Planning Act. Critics of this legislation observed that it coincided with austerity measures that disproportionally affected those living in poverty. In their book *Hope Under Neoliberal Austerity: Responses from Civil Society and Civic Universities* (2021), Simin Davoudi, Mel Steer, Mark Shucksmith, and Liz Todd make connections between the UK's Coalition government's neoliberal austerity policies and civil society, arguing that drastic cuts to local authority services between 2010 and 2016 left local charities and voluntary organisations to provide a safety net for the most vulnerable, including foodbanks (Steer, Davoudi, Shucksmith and Todd, 2021, pp. 1–18). Austerity increased the need for local organisations to take responsibility for social services, but the lack of accountability makes them vulnerable to privatisation by large corporations. The impact of austerity, they suggest, offers one explanation for renewed calls for universities to fulfil a civic role. A refreshed interest in civic role of arts organisations, initiated in 2016 by the Calouste Gulbenkian Foundation, represents a similar ambition to support local neighbourhoods. As Jenny Hughes argues in Chapter 3, civic cultures can be exclusionary as well as radically disruptive.

Theatres discussed in this chapter all grapple with changing relationships between local audiences and local theatre-making. They represent different parts of the theatre economy (amateur, professional, and community) and illustrate how localism is played out in response to their towns' circumstances. Farnham in Surrey is home to Farnham Maltings, an arts organisation that serves as a regional hub for professional theatre-makers and communities in towns across South East England. Slough's diverse and multiple communities show how local and global cultures can come together in a community programme co-curated with professional producers and supported by public funds. Wallingford in Oxfordshire is a market town with a volunteer-run theatre that is a major local asset, sustained by the generous commitment of townspeople. Everywhere I visited, I heard the kind of 'deep stories' that, Arlie Russell Hochschild suggested, define a sense of selfhood, place, and values (Hochschild, 2016, p. 237). My encounters with each town started on foot, walking in the streets, town squares, shopping malls, and markets as well as visiting theatres and venues for performance. Walking offered time to think and feel, to explore what Rebecca Solnit memorably described as 'an invisible crop of memories and associations' that give a place a sense of meaning (Solnit, 2001, p. 13).

Crafting stories: Regional encounters

Unlike some other English regions, the South East does not enjoy a particularly strong sense of local identity, and the cultural provision in its many towns tends to be overlooked due to their proximity to London. Yet many people living in the region are closely affiliated with their towns, and audiences and artists are increasingly looking for creative opportunities in their local area. Farnham, with a population of around 27,000 and quick rail links to London, describes itself as a craft town. It has been home to a specialist art college since 1871 (now University for the Creative Arts), and The Maltings Theatre and Craft Studios has served the town for over 50 years. The Maltings receives regular funding from Arts Council England as a National Portfolio Organisation as well as financial support from local authorities and charities for specific projects. In this section I am interested in who becomes storytellers and whose stories are told, and how theatres and performances contribute to enriching and diversifying the region's cultural life.

Craft is part of Farnham's heritage, and it was clear on my walk through the town that its market stalls and craft shops continue to support local makers. The Maltings' atmospheric buildings were once a tannery and its malts served the local brewery, but today it provides Farnham residents with a lively mix of performances, festivals, and participatory programmes, and it enjoys an international reputation for its creative collaborations. The town's streetscape also commemorates its political history, and in 2016 a bronze statue of the pamphleteer and writer William Cobbett was unveiled on Long Bridge close to the public park. Born in Farnham in 1763 and buried in St Andrew's Church in 1835, William Cobbett's statue depicts him on horseback – a reference to his book *Rural Rides*, first published as pamphlets between 1822 and 1830. *Rural Rides* (1886) captures his journey across the South East region, where he observed agricultural life and documented the living conditions of the poor in its towns and villages. Cobbett was an energetic campaigner against the capitalist exploitation of the rural poor who inspired thinkers on the political Left – including Karl Marx and Raymond Williams – but he also defended the slave trade by rehearsing the racist argument that black slaves were better treated than white factory workers. His views found favour with the English poor, particularly those who felt that the political élite were out of touch with their constituents, dishonest, and corrupt. His birthplace is now a pub that hosts regular live music, and inside the church I found leaflets about the local foodbank and other forms of local aid. As I traced his footprints through the town, I wondered what Cobbett would make of today's political climate.

The Maltings plays a leading role in the South East's cultural economy, and their programmes reflect an egalitarian commitment to the cultural expression of towns and underserved communities across the region. Gavin Stride, Artistic Director of Farnham Maltings from 2002 to 2022, explains his vision:

> One of the things I think we're particularly interested about in the South East is towns and small communities. I'm really curious about how those communities express who they are, what cultural events do they use, particularly in places where there isn't an arts centre or a theatre, and how to we help and share with them those models of expression.
>
> (Gavin Stride)[1]

Farnham Maltings programmes illustrate how this ambition comes to life. *House* is a network of 160 venues across the region, many situated in towns, which provides a regional infrastructure for innovative touring theatre. *Caravan assembly* extends this approach on a national scale by curating a biennial platform for new performances, held at the Brighton

Festival in 2022 with a focus on social distancing practices with communities. *No Strings Attached* is an annual programme that supports young people in the South East region to make their first piece of professional theatre, aided by a small grant, training, and mentoring.

The Maltings' *New Popular* programme resonates with John McGrath's advocacy for localism, first published in 1981 as part of his manifesto for a popular theatre, *A Good Night Out*. His values have stood the test of time:

> Localism, not only of material, but also a *sense of identity* with the performer... a sense that he or she cares enough about being in that place with that audience and actually knows something about them.
>
> (McGrath, 1996, p. 58, italics original)

Funded by Esmé Fairbairn Foundation, *New Popular* reimagines McGrath's ambition for the twenty-first century. Initiated in 2020, this five-year programme supports theatre-makers from under-represented populations in the region. Its inspirational producer Katy Potter describes how it worked in the first year:

> We wanted to put our ambition out there and see how artists responded. So we put out a Call for artists interested in putting audiences at the very heart of their work and its creation, and to be mischievous about where their work might take place.
>
> (Katy Potter)[2]

As a result, artists created interactive performances in shopping centres, beaches, pubs, and football clubs, using rich variety of participatory forms. Gavin Stride summarises his intention to 'shift how people think and feel about theatre and performance', particularly in places where people don't think theatre is for them.[3]

Farnham Maltings' collaboration with Buckinghamshire libraries extends this ambition by developing long-term regional partnerships with organisations not normally associated with theatre. Libraries are among the few remaining civic amenities in English towns; they are recognisably local authority run and offer information about council services as well as the opportunity to borrow books. Writing about libraries in New York, Eric Klinenberg describes them as 'social infrastructure in action' because they offer free social spaces for local people to gather, with 'open access to shared culture and heritage' and activities that foster convivial networks (Klinenberg, 2018, pp. 37–39). Klinenberg's perception resonates in with libraries in England. Lasana Shabazz, a queer interdisciplinary artist who grew up in the Buckinghamshire town of High Wycombe, returned to their hometown to lead a project called *I am Wycombe* in local libraries. Their work began with a question:

> A library is made of hundreds if not thousands of stories but who decides what stories are valid and get remembered?
> (Lasana Shabazz)[4]

The question is apposite; artists' residences invite local people to share stories in new ways, taking people away from their immediate surroundings by creating moments of magic in the quotidian surroundings of a library.

On a wet December day in 2021 I arrived at Chesham Library, Buckinghamshire for Marie Klimis' immersive storytelling experience, *I am a Bird*, produced by Farnham Maltings. The library is housed in an unassuming 1970s municipal building on the edge of Sainsbury's car park and, as I entered there was a display about local history on my left, and a hand sanitiser on my right. I was greeted by artist Marie Klimis, and her instructions were simple – listen to the story unfold on my phone's headset and follow the trail via QR codes around the library. I was guided first to the children's book section where I met a young bird beginning its migration journey from West Africa to London. The storytelling was interactive, and after each scene I was invited to decide the next stage of the bird's journey. My route took me to sections of the library I might not otherwise encounter, transporting me into a fictional world, and inviting me to see the library's book collection in new ways. Twenty-two miniature installations hidden in the library shelves were part of the performance aesthetic; a tiny paper egg was concealed in a hollowed-out book and a beautiful origami map of the bird's flight nested between a book's covers. The story was rich in metaphor, inviting empathy as the bird was trafficked across the sea and found hungry and homeless in London. These beautiful miniature artworks created a new kind of social space for audiences; literature scholar Susan Stewart's words are appositive here:

> The social space of the miniature book might be seen as the social space, in miniature, of all books: the book as talisman to the body and emblem of the self; the book as microcosm and macrocosm; the book as commodity and knowledge, fact and fiction.
> (Stewart, 1993, p. 41).

Sally Walters, manager of Chesham Library, likened the performative experience of *I am a Bird* to the imaginative process of reading. Becoming immersed in the story was close to being captivated by a book, she suggested, where 'you're seeing the story in your mind, and you're making images that feel real'.[5] The story of the migrant bird was gentle, moving and profoundly political. Writer Ali Smith, Patron of Refugee Tales, describes the power of stories to inspire other-regarding emotions:

> Story has always been a welcoming-in, is always one way or another a hospitable meeting of the needs of others, and a porous artform where sympathy and empathy are only the beginning of things.
>
> (Smith)[6]

I am a bird represented a meeting place of two hospitable places – the social space of the library and the welcoming-in of the story itself. The juxtaposition between the everyday environment of the library and the imagined story folded two worlds together, each shaping a sense of place. Story and library occupied a space simultaneously within and beyond the local, and I was left hoping that engaging with the miniature world of *I am a bird* would quietly contribute to making migrants feel welcome.

Figure 2.1 *I am a bird*, Artist, Marie Klimis. Photograph by permission of Neil Marshment

At the heart of the project in Buckinghamshire libraries lies The Maltings' commitment to regional towns as places to create and host innovative theatre. Its success depends on the craft and skill of producers. Sally Walters valued the partnership with Farnham Maltings and appreciated the producers' ability to imagine new kinds of theatre in library settings. In conversation, Gavin Stride directed me towards Peter MacFayden's book about local democracy in the Somerset town of Frome, *Flatpack Democracy* (2014). The book champions local agency, creativity, and the power of the political imagination, and seems to capture the spirit of The Maltings' programmes in the region's towns. This approach aims to expand cultural horizons and enable venues to gain confidence and take risks. In Chesham library, the collaboration with Farnham Maltings showed librarians what is possible, and since *I am a Bird* other local artists have taken residences. As Sally Walters remarked, 'We can do anything now' (Walters, 2022).

The relationship between local agency, cultural organisations, local theatres, and towns across the region contributes to narratives of place, inviting audiences to hear stories in ways that are hospitable, empathetic, and outward facing. Writing about locality as a structure of feeling, Appadurai argues that the imagination has both social and cultural significance:

> The production of locality is as much a work of the imagination as a work of material social construction... Of course locality has a spatial dimension, a scalar dimension, a material dimension and a kind of embodied dimension, but I want to infuse them with the idea that in the world in which we live the imagination actually can reach into multiple scales and spaces and forms and possibilities. These then can become part of the toolkit through which the structure of feeling can be produced locally.
> (Appadurai, 2010, p. 250)

In these terms, the imagination is a social practice rather than an individualised faculty of mind and, as such, it is integral to producing local places. This means that the arts, including theatre and performance, not only have gathering powers that bring people together convivially in towns, but they can also enable stable narratives of place to be disrupted and re-imagined. To understand this further, I returned to Slough, known as the most diverse town in the UK, where I have worked with schools and arts organisations for nearly twenty years.

Co-producing local stories

As a post-industrial town, Slough has a history of welcoming migrants who have contributed to its distinctive identity. Welsh, Polish, South Asian, Caribbean, Somalian, and Romanian settlers made their homes in Slough, each community representing layers of historic injustices created by poverty, war, and colonialism, and there are currently over 150 languages currently spoken in a population of 160,000. Appadurai's description of locality as 'globally produced' is particularly apt for Slough, where affective international relationships and global cultural flows are interwoven in the fabric of local life (Appadurai, 2008, p. 188). In this section, I shall discuss *Home Slough*, funded by Arts Council England's Creative People and Places scheme. Initiated in 2012, Creative People and Places focusses on investment in parts of the country where participation in the arts is significantly below the national average. Designated as a priority area for Arts Council England's investment 2021–2024, Slough is grappling with how its multiple communities are best served by its cultural provision and how participation in the arts might increase.

Slough illustrates the complexity of crafting a local arts programme in a town where its residents enjoy multiple global affiliations. Slough is justifiably proud that its elected representatives have made political history; Lydia Simmonds became England's first black Mayor in 1984 and Tan Dhesi, elected as Labour MP for Slough in 2017, was the first turbaned Sikh to take a seat in any European Parliament. Since the demise of its factories, Slough has proved attractive to multinational companies, and the town has the highest concentration of corporate headquarters outside of London, including Mars, Blackberry, McAfee, Burger King, Telefonica, and Lego. Few of their executives live in the town, and the local cultural infrastructure illustrates the kind of social inequalities found across the South East region. Windsor and Eton are a short two-mile stroll from Slough, and home to some of the richest and most socially privileged people in the country. Windsor boasts the historic Theatre Royal and Eton College (fees £48,000 per annum) has two theatres for their pupils' exclusive use. Migrant labour made Slough prosperous, but there is also significant deprivation and, in some districts, a third of Slough's children are thought to be living in poverty. Economic dependence on Heathrow airport meant that Slough's residents were particularly badly hit by the pandemic in 2020 and 2021, amplifying existing inequalities and testing local resilience. In July 2021 Slough Borough Council issued a Section 114 Notice which effectively declared the Council bankrupt;

all non-essential spending paused, followed by job losses and cuts to services. Around the same time, the NGO Hope not Hate published a report, *Building Back Resilient: Strengthening communities through the COVID-19 recovery* (2021) which identified Slough as increasingly vulnerable to Far-Right overtures.

Stories of civic, commercial, community, and cultural life are etched on Slough's high street. Slough is undergoing its second wave of regeneration, having been reconstructed in the 1970s when the high street was pedestrianised and the shopping mall built. The 'Heart of Slough' regeneration programme began in 2009, and one of its first capital projects was a new flagship library and cultural centre, The Curve, which opened in 2016. Walking from the railway station to the high street on a grey day in April 2022 it felt strange to see that familiar landmarks had disappeared; the Council's 1970s Brutalist library and a university building designed by the Richard Rogers Partnership had been demolished to make way for housing, offices, and hotels, no doubt aiming to attract commuters served by the new Elizabeth Line with fast travel across London. Signs of Slough's financial problems were visible – weeds were growing in the pavement and overflowing bins – but The Curve itself was well used, and I paused to revisit the local history displays. Slough was once a lively centre of entertainment, and the Beatles famously performed at The Adelphi Theatre in 1963 (now a dilapidated Bingo Hall). As I walked from The Curve, stories of struggle were evident on the street. One big department store had ceased trading in 2017 and another 2020, and their cavernous buildings were empty or filled by discount stores. At this end of the high street, the town felt desolate and unloved. But as I walked further, a different story emerged, one that represented Slough's rich food cultures and its entrepreneurial migrant communities. A family-run Turkish bakery was selling huge wheels of baklava, a Polish supermarket was stacked with Eastern European brands, a green grocer supplied ingredients for South Asian cookery, and a fishmonger sold fish labelled with Tamil names. They captured Slough's independence, and its distinctive fusions of local and global cultures.

Slough may lack the cultural assets of its Windsor and Eton neighbours, but it has rich local cultures, whether they are found in traditions observed at home such as mehndi designs for henna painted hands, or an inspirational film production company Resource Productions that is diversifying the creative industries, or in the UK's only permanent Sikh Art Gallery, curated by volunteers of Guru Maneyo Granth Gurdwara. Not all this activity is captured by official datasets, and Home Slough aims to serve the towns wide-ranging interests by co-curating their programme with local people. The Community Programming Group is an open forum of local volunteers who work with professional producers to ensure that community voices are at the heart of the work. HOME is also an acronym, used to capture the programme's mission:

H = HOME around the High Street offers a programme of public art and events in the town centre;
O = On Your Doorstep is a hyper-local programme in the town's smaller libraries, green spaces and in homes;
M = Make, Do and Mend is a programme based on mutual aid and community wellbeing, engaging audiences and participants in residential care, day centres and sheltered accommodation;
E = Experiment2 Excite supports experimental artists' residences in locations across Slough.

Home Slough's ethos is inclusive, and the programme is designed to bring residents together in ways that celebrate the town's plural identities. The political theorist Chantal Mouffe argued that the emotional and affective qualities of the arts means that they can redefine social relations, particularly, she suggests, when they take place in public spaces outside traditional institutions (Mouffe, 2013, p. 87). But this is not an easy fix, and in the twenty years I worked in Slough I have seen many arts-based initiatives come and go.

One of Home Slough's successful projects during the Covid lockdowns was inspired by the town's culinary culture. The Global Cooking Theatre was a series of on-line cookery workshops and storytelling, co-curated by the Slough Caribbean Forum. The conceit was simple; everyone who signed up was sent a list of affordable ingredients and people cooked the recipe at home under the guidance of local chefs (or Artistic Nutritional Creatives) from different food heritages. While the food was cooking, storytellers and chefs sometimes in traditional costumes – told stories that reflected their cultural background. Europe, South Asia, the Caribbean, and Africa were represented in the programme, and it provided an opportunity for people not only to expand their culinary repertoires but also to learn about each other's food and storytelling cultures.

Connecting communities through stories is a feature of Home Slough, replacing divisive narratives with feelings of hope. A storytelling project, CAMPFIRES, enabled professional storytellers and spoken word artists to co-create stories with a range of local people, including a Polish folklore dance group, members of St Kitts and Nevis Association Slough,

Figure 2.2 Love Slough – *The Dance WE Made* by Casson & Friends. Photographer, Mike Swift

Slough Young Careers, and users of Slough Homeless Our Concern. The Love Slough Festival in March 2022 aminated Slough High Street over a two-week period with drumming from the Dhol Collective, a sound installation of Slough Community voices presented by theatre company Milk Presents and an interactive dance performance, *The Dance WE Made*. In this performance, two Slough-based trainee dancers and two professional dancers from Cassson & Friends performed a dance spontaneously choreographed by members of the public on the high street. Temporarily redefined as a space of creative production as well as consumption, empty shops became spaces for music and art galleries. Writing about the future of town centres, Julian Dobson stressed their social and cultural value, where local stories, shared memories and community activities create a sustainable future: '[t]he way we tell the stories of these places helps to frame our own future' (Dobson, 2015, p. 19).

Home Slough shows how performance in towns negotiates local identities in places of cultural pluralism and heterogeneity, bringing together different communities who may live side-by-side in the town but share little contact. Finding creative connections for people who would not otherwise meet brings challenges, particularly where there are historic tensions have travelled across time and space.

Targeted public funding supports such initiatives and, at best, reciprocity between arts organisations, producers, community groups, local makers, and audiences means that it is not only arts events that are co-created, but the towns themselves.

Making local theatre

> I'm in the audience for Wallingford's annual pantomime at the Corn Exchange, a beautiful theatre in the town's market square. It's towards the end of a two-week sell-out run. There's a feeling of shared anticipation in the auditorium as people from different generations gather for the show.
> (Research Journal, 29 January 2022)

The final town discussed in this chapter is Wallingford, a market town of around 8000 inhabitants in South Oxfordshire. The Corn Exchange drew me to Wallingford and, unlike the other theatres described in this chapter, it operates largely without public subsidy as a self-sustaining, independent, not-for-profit organisation. The remarkable story of how the Corn Exchange became a centre for the arts illustrates deep connections between the town and its theatre; in the 1970s members of the local amateur theatre company, the Sinodun Players, transformed a derelict shell into a stunning theatre with their own hands. Corn Exchange Wallingford Ltd is now a thriving member of the Little Theatre Guild, a national organisation for independent amateur theatre companies that own, run, and programme their own theatre buildings. The Corn Exchange and the Sinodun Players were given the Queen's Award for Voluntary Service in 2020, nominated by Deputy Lieutenants for Oxfordshire Miranda Markham and Kate Tiller, who commented that the award recognised 'how a traditional local organisation can transform itself and develop into a key community asset for the 21st century'.[7] This citation challenges the stereotype of amateur theatres as self-serving, and I was interested to learn more about the place of the Corn Exchange in the cultural life of the town.

I wasn't sure what to expect on my first visit to Wallingford. The town is rich in heritage and is known for two things: its medieval heritage and its association with crime fiction. Wallingford played an important role in the Middle Ages; it was one of Alfred the Great's fortified 'new towns' in the Saxon era and, following the Norman conquest, it became an important royal residence with a showy castle to rival Windsor. The Corn Exchange, built in 1856 to serve local farmers, is indebted to Wallingford's medieval history; Henry 11 granted Wallingford a Charter of Liberties in 1155 that gave them the right to hold regular markets. Its status as a market town with good river transport to London secured its place as a centre of local commerce and, although no longer a major centre of agriculture, the town square still hosts weekly 'charter markets'. The Corn Exchange connects its market town heritage with its other claim-to-fame, crime fiction. Agatha Christie was a long-time resident, living in the town from 1934 to her death in 1976, and she served as president of the Sinodun Players from 1951 to 1976. Wallingford is also a main location for the long-running TV series *Midsomer Murders*, and early episodes regularly featured cameos from local amateur actors. The dramatic tension of detective stories often depends on the shock of crime in closely-knit communities, and they paint a picture of towns that are affluent, cultural conservative, and a little inward-looking. This fiction of a homogenised culture was fuelled by the co-creator and producer of *Midsomer Murders*, Brian True-May, who was suspended in 2011 when he refused to cast black actors, offering the uncomfortably racist view that an all-white cast would maintain the fictional town as the 'last bastion of Englishness'.[8] Television and tourism theatricalises places, but fictionalised images are often far from reality. The Corn Exchange, the marketplace, the castle ruins, the Thames path, and the ninth century street layout promised a town layered with stories.

Figure 2.3 Wallingford Corn Exchange on the market square. Photographer, Helen Nicholson

Walking became a tool to think. Over the next few months, I walked with townspeople through the market square, on streets, through public parks, and along pathways, each offering insights into their 'personalised trails' around the town. I was shown round churches, old pubs, and the Corn Exchange itself, hearing the deep stories that create attachments to place and enabling me to see Wallingford from different perspectives. Wallingford's Mayor Marcus Harris served as one of my guides; he is the latest in an unbroken line of Mayors that can be traced by name to 1231. Marcus Harris was a child actor – he played Julian in a TV adaptation of Enid Blyton's *The Famous Five* in the late 1970s – and he remains a popular local performer, member of the Sinodun Players, and relishes the ceremonial aspects of his office. His description of Wallingford shows that he cares deeply about the town, the place he has lived all his life:

> So what is Wallingford? I'd say Wallingford is the home of independent retailers, pubs and bars. This gives us a different feel from towns nearby. We don't court the tourists, and unlike Henley we don't have a big field near the river to put on events. So the community fill the space, and the community shops in the shops. People like to spend their time here – and the Corn Exchange is a big part of that. I think that's one reason why this town has a heartbeat, and that's the beauty of it.
>
> (Harris)[9]

Wallingford is represented by the Green Party on local councils which encourage sustainable living and local shopping; in addition to a local bookshop, hardware store, independent coffee shops, and family-run food shops, there are several zero waste shops. Wallingford's independent spirit is also evident in its cultural life, represented not only by the Corn Exchange but also Bunkfest, an annual free music, dance, and beer festival. Bunkfest was founded in 2002 by two local folk music enthusiasts in the pub, and by 2022 had grown to include world music and dance attracting over 30,000 visitors. Bunkfest brings a Glastonbury vibe to Wallingford's public spaces for a weekend each September, and its family-friendly feel at the first post-pandemic festival in 2022 brought together local people and visitors, all welcomed by Mayor Harris, supported by local volunteers from across the town. Wallingford is a town that enjoys performance, and there is also a calendar of social and cultural events that animate the town's public spaces at other times of year: the cycling festival; classic car rally; the summer street carnival; the bonfire night fireworks, and the arrival of Santa's sleigh are all organised by volunteers.

Local Theatres 29

Figure 2.4 Wallingford's Mayor, Marcus Harris, opening Bunkfest 2022. Photographer: Helen Nicholson

Local amenities and its convivial atmosphere make Wallingford attractive to housing developers who market the town's lifestyle to lockdown-weary Londoners seeking outside space, country living, and community spirit. Wallingford's 2021 Neighbourhood Plan recommended building additional 30,000 homes before 2035, but the scale of the expansion was controversial. Environmental activist Sue Roberts, who represented Wallingford on South Oxfordshire District Council, was a vocal opponent. She described plans for new-build housing in apocalyptic terms:

> Nature is in collapse. We are down to our last few insects. Once we have lost the pollinators there will be no fruit, few vegetables … just the wind-pollinated grains; just bread to eat. Wildlife cannot

survive in the fragments of space between the roads and the concrete. This housing adds to global heating.

(Roberts, 2021).

Roberts' legal challenge failed, and Wallingford's Neighbourhood Plan was overwhelmingly approved by a local referendum in May 2021. But maintaining a sense of community in market towns facing in-migration is a continued challenge, as Trevor Hart and Neil Powe point out in their book *Market Towns* (2007), citing social inclusion, affordable housing for local young people, changing age-profile, and access to schools and health services high on the agenda. Marcus Harris, who had initially opposed the housing plans, recognised these challenges, but also valued the energy that new people were bringing to the town:

> Are they changing Wallingford? No, not yet. And I don't think they will. There are thousands and thousands of new homes, and thousands of new people moving to the community and the area. But once you look past the loss of green fields, then you look at it and you say, here are a bunch of people who are choosing to live in Wallingford. And they love it here – they are making a real contribution. It's bringing great new people to the community, and it will be great for our bars, pubs, shops and entertainment venues.
>
> (Harris, 2021)

In this optimistic version of expansion, integration into local life is key to successful growth, with new residents boosting the local economy and bringing increased social and cultural capital to the town. Writing about new housing in market towns, Susannah Gunn and Neil Powe argue that in-migrants often contribute to voluntary and community activities, but they also observe that local organisations can become dominated by 'new, mainly middle-class, arrivals' (Gunn and Powe, 2007, p. 95). Mayor Harris was alert to this challenge and keen to see an inclusive Wallingford; he welcomed all new residents, including those who bring 'a more multicultural feel' to the town and spoke warmly about a popular new pub landlady who introduced a menu that reflected her Jamaican heritage. There is a fine balance to be struck here between integration and assimilation, as Jon Garland and Neil Chakraborti explain. Their research on rural racism relates to village life, but their findings might also be relevant to rural towns:

> [An] important aspect of the 'process of acceptance' into rural communities for minority ethnic people; it is a process of assimilation,

rather than integration. Often it appears that white rural communities expect minority ethnic households to adopt the pre-existing (and essentially white English) cultural, social and religious norms' that characterise village life.

(Garland and Chakraborti, 2011. p. 128)

Garland and Chakraborti found that there is often an expectation that black and global majority residents need to 'fit in' to existing community activities to become accepted. In the 2011 census, the population of Wallingford was overwhelmingly white (over 95%), and there may be lessons to be learned from their research as the town expands and narratives of place evolve.

The current custodians of the Corn Exchange are alert to the pace of change in Wallingford and the opportunities and challenges it brings. The story of the Sinodun Players' relationship with the Corn Exchange provides a compelling insight into how this local theatre has adapted to changing times. The Sinodun Players was founded in 1948 by Frances Curtis, a Gaiety Girl who married a local farmer, and their early performances were in farm outbuildings. By 1970, they had outgrown all available performance spaces and were looking for a permanent space in the town. The Corn Exchange had been derelict for almost a decade and, aided by an anonymous loan of £20,000, the Players bought the building in 1975 and embarked on an energetic campaign of fund-raising, planning applications, and renovation work. It takes confidence to lead such a risky project, but it captured the town's imagination, and many local people volunteered their labour, skills, and expertise for the project. Photographs documenting the building work capture volunteers up ladders, on roofs, and carrying steel girders, an alarming number of whom worked without hard hats or steel-toe-capped boots. Within three years they had converted the building into a beautiful 175-seat theatre and cinema, officially opened by Sir Peter Hall in 1978 (then director of the National Theatre). Over forty-five years later many of these brave volunteers were still involved in the theatre, and it was moving to hear stories about its significance throughout their lives. John Warburton joined the Players in 1969, and described the different roles he had undertaken over his lifetime:

> I was one of the half a dozen people who turned the key to this derelict building in 1975 and worked for three years until it was opened by Sir Peter Hall. I put in the planning application for

this, but we had no details, we had no money, and no nothing. I remember talking to the conservation officer and putting in five sheets of A4 paper... a great guy – he accepted it. I've done a lot a since – I was a general manager for 21 years, and since then I've been cinema manager and dozens and dozens of plays. I've even done pantomime. There's not a thing I haven't done.

(Warburton)[10]

As John Warburton and his contemporaries testified, there are many opportunities to contribute, both on and off-stage, which gives theatre-making wide appeal. The fabric and facilities have been improved over time, and a lifetime of shared interests has created strong social bonds. In 2020 the town rallied again to the Corn Exchange's defence, this time successfully campaigning against plans to convert the neighbouring bank into flats. Housing would inevitably curtail noisy activities in the auditorium, significantly limiting activity and reducing its cultural and socio-economic value to the town. The campaign was supported by the Theatre Trust and, as town that is conscious of its carbon footprint, this led to discussions about how the Corn Exchange might make greater use of the green technologies they advocate.

The scale of Wallingford has been key to the Corn Exchange's success, sustained by its varied programme, enthusiastic volunteers, and low-ticket prices. The building is a major asset, and although long-standing locals know it well, new residents can assume it is a private club for members rather than an inspirational and creative and cultural hub for the whole town. There is a familiar double-bind here; people who have worked together for many years bring their love and deep knowledge to the theatre, but it can make the place appear introverted, however outward-looking and friendly they intend to be. Members of the Little Theatre Guild are alert to this perception and are actively exploring new ways to appear more inclusive, informed by the research of Anne-marie Greene, Artistic Director of the Criterion Theatre in Earlson Coventry.[11] Similarly, although longstanding members value intergenerational friendships and meeting people outside their immediate social circles, joining an established group can be intimating. One member described her experiences as a new resident:

I want somewhere local I can call my arthouse. I want to wander in and see something without feeling self-conscious. But the first time I came the door was closed and thought it must be a private club and I didn't come back for ten years. I was brought back by NT Live as I was missing feeling part of London's cultural life.[12]

Catering for different tastes is important, particularly as the town evolves, and the Corn Exchange is well-placed to attract wide local audiences. Its programme is lively and eclectic, including performances that include well-known comedians, local bands, spoken word poets, and the Sinodun Players' own productions. There is strong local loyalty for the Sinodun Players' annual pantomime, and its inexpensive tickets and high production values are appreciated by family audiences. Live streaming from major cultural organisations including NT Live and Northern Ballet brings in theatre audiences, and those seeking more up-beat musical entertainment appreciate bands and live-streamed concerts. Local fans of the band Take That asked the Corn Exchange to live-stream their concert which gave them a good night out, and although bar takings were boosted by the sale of many small bottles of prosecco, not everyone in the building appreciated the audience's spontaneous on-stage dancing. Young people's choice of film is programmed once a month, and local schools and organisations – including Bunkfest – use the Corn Exchange for their activities. The Players support a variety of events in the town – in 2017, for example, set-builders constructed a combustible 24-foot model of the Houses of Parliament for Wallingford's charity bonfire night celebrations. It is, however, involvement in making theatre that brings feelings of ownership and a deep sense of belonging, whether this involves caring for the fabric of the building, or as theatre-makers, set builders, costume-makers, projectionists, ushers, and the many other voluntary roles John Warburton described. His generation leaves an inspirational legacy for the next generation of creative talent who will in turn add to the building's biography, using their imaginations to develop new art forms and ways of working, or by simply doing some things differently.

As Wallingford expands, attracting new people to the Corn Exchange's activities is an important step towards re-shaping its cultural vision for the mid-twenty-first century. Gloria Wright, who led the successful 2020 campaign against housing development, became Chair of the Corn Exchange in 2021 following a period of office as Chair of the Sinodun Players. A talented actor and director, she describes the Players as an inclusive company.[13] Small adjustments have increased accessibility and sociability – people with disabilities have been encouraged to perform and, as Covid restrictions lifted, costume-makers appreciated sewing together on machines in newly placed workshops rather that making costumes alone at home. Reassessing the Corn Exchange's contribution to Wallingford's nighttime economy led to a partnership with The Old Post Office, a local restaurant across the town square, which offered 15% discount for ticketholders. Creating a good night out proved mutually beneficial when the Corn Exchange showed the newly released James Bond film in 2021. First-night audiences dressed up and enjoyed Bond-themed cocktails before crossing the square to the Corn Exchange. The run was a great success, although some newer audience members wanted even more from their cinema experience, leading Gloria Wright to conclude that 'we really need to look at popcorn'.

Beyond debates about popcorn and prosecco there lies a vision for a revitalised creative and cultural hub at the centre of the town that attracts new residents to get involved. Professional directors and artists are already drawn to the beautiful, well-equipped theatre, and by 2021 energetic conversations were taking place about how the Corn Exchange might become a space to experiment with new artforms, with dreams of expanded facilities including virtual reality (VR) workshops, recording studios, pop-up events, artist residences, and galleries that create an art-house atmosphere and serve as a creative hub for emergent artists and local people.[14] This imagined future is ambitious, but the town's expansion provides a realistic opportunity for the Corn Exchange to change, as Gloria Wright describes:

> Wallingford is growing, the number of houses is growing. Let's acknowledge that transition. Now and the next five years are some of the most challenging, interesting, and important years that we've faced because we are the generation that are going to have to make a big leap from amateur to semi-professional. We have to say ok, this where we are now, and we're going to take that risk. We need think about employing someone full-time so that the door is never closed during the day.
>
> (Wright)[15]

Furthermore, demand for local cultural activities is likely to rise if homeworking increases and the sociability of the workplace is lost. To respond to changing times, the Corn Exchange's leadership knows they will need the same level of vision and confidence as their predecessors who converted the building, and this requires volunteers who are not afraid of business-plans, spreadsheets, and large budgets. Without their expertise and enthusiasm, freely given, this community asset would simply not exist. The challenge is to ensure that this dynamic venue continues to benefit the town in the future, making an inspirational space where anyone seeking cultural and creative opportunities can find their place.

Local Theatres 35

Figure 2.5 Sign on Corn Exchange inviting new people to volunteer, September 2022. Photographer: Helen Nicholson

Making an inclusive theatre in a relatively small town is perhaps more difficult than it might appear. There is a myth that people living in picturesque towns are socially privileged, captured in Raymond Williams' pithy phrase: 'Flowers and privilege; factory smoke and democracy' (Williams, 1973, p. 196). There is, however, hidden poverty experienced by Wallingford's residents, as Marcus Harris described:

> We have some serious pockets of deprivation, and we certainly have some communities that have significant deprivation-related issues within them. A lot of people don't think it or see it, but we have those challenges like many, many other places.
>
> (Harris, 2021)

Marcus Harris introduced me to Gareth Lloyd-Jones who is senior pastor of Wallingford's Ridgeway Community Church, a few doors down the road from the Corn Exchange, and attended by a large, diverse, and multi-racial congregation. The church began Wallingford foodbank and Community Fridge over ten years ago, run entirely by volunteers with food donated by local people. It was intended to meet short-term need, but by 2022 it was feeding over 200 local people each month, most of whom were in full-time low-paid work and ineligible for benefits. The church also supports vulnerable young people who live or attend school in the town, and their Beacon Youth Project is partly funded by Wallingford Town Council. Karen Whiting is the church's youth worker, and she observed that assumptions about the town often mask the very real challenges young people face:

> People assume that we don't have problems because Wallingford is a nice-looking town. One of the challenges as a youth worker, working in a town like Wallingford, is that so much goes on behind closed doors and the difficulties with young people are hidden.
> (Whiting)[16]

Few of the town's cultural amenities appeal to these young people, Karen Whiting explained, and they prefer the vibe of Didcot's multiplex to Wallingford's Corn Exchange. She described how they gather on streets to avoid the challenges poverty brings to home life, where they can easily acquire reputations for anti-social behaviour. Karen Whiting sees her role as providing support and activities that increase young people's sense of self-worth and raise their aspirations. Rural poverty is particularly stigmatising in places that are considered affluent and, as sociologist Imogen Tyler has described, stigma leads to shame that is intense and personally felt, 'it infiltrates, pieces and deflates your sense of yourself' (Tyler, 2020, p. 239). Ridgeway Community Church regard this work as part of their Christian mission, and although I remain troubled by an evangelical church taking over services once provided by the welfare state, the care and compassion I witnessed for local people in need was profoundly moving.

Wallingford's commitment to environmental sustainability, an independent and localised economy, strongly engaged voluntarism, and a rich cultural life is part of its identity. The town also represents a constellation of contemporary challenges: the effects of climate change, housing and over-development, the social implications of in-migration, the use of public spaces, cultural and heritage assets, the localised effects of poverty and reduction in the welfare state. The theatre is evolving in ways that underline how the local is inextricably bound up with wider national and international issues. It also illustrates local agency, and how a town's cultural life is continually changing in response to new circumstances. Making an inspiring and sustainable local theatre involves finding new ways to serve the whole town's community and building on the success of generations of townspeople for whom the theatre represents a deep story of enduring commitment and love.

Performance and the paradox of localism

At the centre of this chapter there is a paradox which affects how theatres in towns are perceived and experienced. On one hand, localism is associated with cultural conservatism and resistance to change. On the other, localism fosters agency, resilience, hope, and communities of care. Theatres in towns negotiate this contested space, and performances often balance localised place-based identities with artistic repertoires that invite alternative ways of seeing. Practical choices about places and spaces for performance, programming, and repertoire illustrate this dilemma, and in each town discussed in this chapter I heard animated conversations about whose stories are told and whose voices are represented in cultural decision-making. Theatres in towns make a significant contribution to producing local cultural life, a process which, according to Appadurai, 'requires agency, purpose, vision and design' (Appadurai, 2010, p. 250).

One intriguing aspect of Appadurai's theory of locality as a structure of feeling is that it is both affective and performative; it depends on creativity, improvision and imagination. The social imagination, in Appadurai's terms, is one way to unfix stable notions of place and infuse locality with wider, global perspectives:

> [T]he horizons of globality, through media and the work of the imagination and migration, can become part of the material through which specific groups of actors can envision, project, design and produce whatever kind of local feeling they wish to produce.
> (Appadurai, 2010, p. 250)

It follows, then, that performance has potential to bring an imagined 'local feeling' into practice on the streets, town squares, libraries, shopping malls and in the theatre. Artists, theatre-makers, and creative producers, who are skilled in the production of feeling, have a particular place in navigating the localism paradox in ways that are inclusive and outward-looking.

In this chapter I have sought to understand theatre's contribution to towns across South East England, examining the paradox of localism that is experienced in many different parts of the world through this setting. There is a myth that the cultural interests of people in the region are satisfied by theatres in cities; high-ticket prices in London and transport costs mean that they mainly serve affluent audiences who already possess specific forms of cultural capital. Overcoming the localism paradox and creating inclusive theatres in towns requires both artistic vision and investment in the local cultural infrastructure, including funding for towns' theatres, coherent opportunities for cultural participation and artistic projects that extend local horizons. The scale of towns suggests that sharing knowledge across sectors and communities, including co-producing programmes and co-creating theatre, is one way to build a sustainable cultural life. Amateur companies and volunteer-run independent theatres often have long and deep-rooted relationships with people in their towns, and their knowledge benefits professionals seeking to strengthen local relationships. Reciprocally, professional producers and theatre-makers can create new opportunities for local theatre-makers and audiences by expanding their artistic repertoires, introducing new ideas, and engaging communities – particularly those without prior experience in theatre – who may not consider joining an established amateur company. Everywhere I visited, I heard conversations about what kind of town local people aspired to create and how theatre and performance might contribute to local cultural life. If locality is performed – as a spatial, affective, and material practice – theatre is one way to understand how narratives of place and identity become produced, challenged, and embodied.

Notes

1 Gavin Stride, in Paul Hodson's film: *The Future is Unwritten*. https://farnhammaltings.com/artists-and-makers/theatre/producing/new-popular. Accessed 13 January 2022
2 Katy Potter, in in Paul Hodson's film: *The Future is Unwritten*. https://farnhammaltings.com/artists-and-makers/theatre/producing/new-popular. Accessed 21 January 2022
3 https://farnhammaltings.com/artists-and-makers/theatre/producing/new-popular. Accessed 21 January 2022
4 Lasana Shabazz, cited discussing their work in I am Wycombe. https://www.buckscc.gov.uk/news-libraries/i-am-wycombe/. Accessed 24 February 2022
5 Interview with Sally Walters, Chesham library, January 11, 2022. All related quotations from this interview.
6 Ali Smith, cited in https://www.refugeetales.org/about. Accessed 20 November 2021
7 https://www.oxfordmail.co.uk/news/19451140.wallingford-theatre-group-awarded-highest-award-voluntary-groups/.
8 This event is analysed by Tiffany Bergin, who describes it as an exercise in 'wilful nostalgia' (2013, p. 89)

9 Interview with Mayor Marcus Harris, 20 September 2021, Wallingford. All related quotations from this interview.
10 John Warburton. Focus group at the Corn Exchange, Wallingford. 27 November 2021
11 Greene learned that local people of colour felt conspicuous if they were the only non-white person in the audience and were unlikely to return. Research shared at The Little Theatre Guild Conference, 14 May 2022, Southport Little Theatre.
12 Member of Corn Exchange, focus group at the Corn Exchange, Wallingford. 27 November 2021
13 Interview with Gloria Wright, Wallingford, 13 August 2021
14 Members of Corn Exchange, focus group at the Corn Exchange, Wallingford. 27 November 2021
15 Gloria Wright, focus group at the Corn Exchange, Wallingford. 27 November 2021
16 Karen Whiting, interview at Ridgway Church, Wallingford. 20 October 2021

References

Appadurai, A. (2008). *Modernity at Large: Cultural Dimensions of Globalisation*. Minneapolis: University of Minnesota Press.
Appadurai, A. (2010). 'The Right to Participate in the Work of the Imagination' in Whybrow, H. (eds.), *Performance and the Contemporary City: An Interdisciplinary Reader*. Basingstoke: Palgrave Macmillan, pp. 249–259.
Bergin, T. (2013). 'Identity and Nostalgia in a Globalised World: Investigating the International Popularity of Midsomer Murders', *Crime, Media, Culture*, 9(1), pp. 83–99.
Buckinghamshire County Council, (2021). *I am Wycombe*. Available at: https://www.buckscc.gov.uk/news-libraries/i-am-wycombe (Accessed 24 February 2022).
Cobbett, W. (1886). *Rural Rides*. London: Reeves & Turner.
Dobson, J. (2015). *How to Save Our Town Centres*. Bristol: Polity Press.
Farnham Maltings Programmes. (2022). Available at: https://farnhammaltings.com/artists-and-makers/theatre/producing/new-popular (Accessed 13 January 2022).
Fowler, C. (2020). *Green Unpleasant Land*. Leeds: Peepal Tree Press.
Garland, J. and Chakraborti, N. (2011). 'Another Country? Community, Belonging and Exclusion in Rural England' in Chakraborti, N. and Garland, J. (eds.), *Rural Racism*. London: Routledge, pp. 122–140.
Gauntlett, D. (2011). *Making Is Connecting: The Social Meaning of Creativity, Form DIY and Knitting to YouTube and Web 2.0*. Cambridge: Polity Press.
Gunn, S. and Powe, N. (2007). 'Capacity vs. Need: Exploring Regional Differences in Housing provision' in Powe, N., Hart, T. and Shaw, T. (eds.), *Market Towns: Roles Challenges and Prospects*. London: Routledge, pp. 93–104.
Hart, T. and Powe, N. (2007). 'Market Towns: Roles, Challenges and Prospects' in Powe, N., Hart, T. and Shaw, T. (eds.), *Market Towns: Roles Challenges and Prospects*. London: Routledge, pp. 148–156.

Hochschild, A. R. (2016). *Strangers in Their Own Land: Anger and Mourning on the American Right*. New York: The New Press.
Hopeful Towns. (2021). *Building Back Resilient Strengthening Communities Through the Covid-19 Recovery*. London: Hope Not Hate Charitable Trust.
Hopkins, R. (2013). *The Power of Just Doing Stuff*. Cambridge: Green Books.
Ingold, T. (2011). *Being Alive: Essays on Movement, Knowledge and Description*. London: Routledge.
Klinenberg, E. (2018). *Palaces for the People: How to Build a More Equal and United Society*. London: Bodley Head.
Localism Act. (2011). Available at: https://www.legislation.gov.uk/ukpga/2011/20/pdfs/ukpga_20110020_en.pdf (Accessed 2 November 2022).
MacFayden, P. (2014). *Flatpack Democracy: A DIY Guide to Independent Politics*. Bath: Eco-logic books.
Madanipour, A. and Davoudi, S. (2015). 'Localism: Institutions, Territories, Representations' in Davoudi, S. and Madanipour, A. (eds.), *Reconsidering Localism*. London: Routledge, pp. 11–29.
McGrath, J. (1996). *A Good Night Out: Popular Theatre, Audience, Class and Form*. London: Nick Hern Books.
Mouffe, C. (2013). *Agonistics: Thinking the World Politically*. London: Verso.
Refugee Tales. (2020). *A Welcome from Our Patron, Ali Smith*. Available at: https://www.refugeetales.org/about (Accessed 20 November 2021).
Roach, J. (1996). *Cities of the Dead: Circum-Atlantic Performance*. New York: Columbia University Press.
Roberts, S. (2021). *Yes, the Local Plan is a Disaster for Wallingford*. Available at: https://www.oxfordmail.co.uk/news/19077185.yes-local-plan-disaster-wallingford (Accessed 28 December 2021).
Sanghera, S. (2021). *Empireland: How Imperialism Has Shaped Modern Britain*. London: Viking Press.
Steer, M., Davoudi, S., Shucksmith, M. and Todd, L. (eds.) (2021). *Hope Under Neoliberal Austerity: Responses from Civil Society and Civic Universities*. Bristol: Polity Press.
Stewart, S. (1993). *On Longing: Narratives of the Miniature, the Gigantic, The Souvenir, the Collection*. London: Duke University Press.
Tyler, I. (2020). *Stigma: The Machine of Inequality*. London: Zed Books.
Walmsley, B. (2019). *Audience Engagement in the Performing Arts: A Critical Analysis*. London: Palgrave.
Williams, R. (1973). *The Country and the City*. London: Chatto and Windus.
Williams, A., Goodwin, M. and Cloke, P. (2014). 'Neoliberalism, Big Society, and Progressive Localism', *Environment and Planning A: Economy and Space*, 46 (December 12), pp. 2798–2815.

# 3 Making a Civic Spectacle
Towns for Rent

Jenny Hughes

The courtroom is lit with party lights and glitter ball and adorned with balloons. A party is about to begin. Clusters of chairs and tables surround a performance area in the centre of the room, and sweets and crisps have been distributed. Our host, leather-clad, whip-laden and pony-tailed 'Queen of this court', offers a 'full force' welcome – 'I'm talking no spit, no lube, no poppers, no hand sanitiser, Bareback and raw'. Iconic dance tune, Adventures of Stevie V's 'Dirty Cash (Money Talks)', plays full blast. The opening speech sets the tone – queer, fierce, local – and our host introduces the rules of the game:

> As the grown-ups allegedly run the country, and the homeless spice up their life on the streets, let us pie-eaters stand and Party United, for we are the great unwashed masses, the dirty ones, the nasty ones.
>
> You know what I'm talking about …
>
> Let me explain the game. Right now the front row are being given some Rent Party vouchers … You are going to pay my friends what you deem fit once they've shared their talent and very true stories …
>
> Now, things are about to get very, very interesting, because tonight, for one night only, you are going to sponsor a Wigan life. Because Wigan Lives Matter.

In the performance that follows, five artists from Wigan offer up their wares – song, poem, dance and autobiographical story – and the audience reward them with fake money from small brown envelopes. The game we are invited to play is a contemporary twist on the rent parties of the 1920s Harlem Renaissance, where Black communities, including recent arrivals to Harlem escaping the racist violence of the American South, were facing discriminatory high rents and low wages. By throwing house parties, and charging a small entrance fee for a night of music, dance and food, residents raised income to pay the rent. Migrating across century and continent, this performance-based mutual aid economy inspired a theatrical response to twenty-first century 'Austerity Britain', originally created in 2017 by dancer, choreographer, and drag ball House Mother Darren Pritchard, working with co-writers Cheryl Martin and Sonia Hughes. *Rent Party* was then revived in 2021 by Moving Roots, a collective of arts organisations in England and Wales, including The Old Courts, an arts centre housed in the renovated nineteenth-century law courts in Wigan. The Moving Roots collective came together to pioneer an innovative approach to touring, with a new production of *Rent Party* co-created with artists and communities in each locality.[1]

This chapter shares the story of *Rent Party* in Wigan, a town indelibly marked in the public imagination with the poverty described by Eton-educated socialist, George Orwell, who visited the town in the 1930s and drafted his book, *The Road to Wigan Pier*, in the local free library. Orwell's association of Wigan with poverty turned out to be historically resilient, with Beatrix Campbell's feminist analysis of economic inequality drawing on her visits to the town in the 1980s, and journalist Stephen Armstrong retracing Orwell's steps in his research on the 2011 riots in England (Campbell, 1984; Armstrong, 2012). For Orwell, Wigan was a town dominated by the 'lunar landscape' of the coal industry slag heap: 'a hideous thing, because it is so planless and functionless ... just dumped on the earth, like the emptying of a dustbin' (Orwell, 2001[1937] p. 97–98). The title of his book, repeating a well-worn music hall joke, plays on the dissonance between a seaside resort and the industrial landscapes so distasteful to Orwell. A more even-handed study of Wigan reveals the town as a place where poverty has co-existed with the wealth generated by industrialisation, a source of prosperity that has contracted over the last half-century. This contemporary prospect reveals – in place of a town without form or function – a town with an imaginative civic plan that, like *Rent Party*, queers the logic by which value is constructed and assigned to people and places. And here, art and culture are playing a central role.

I start and end this chapter with *Rent Party*, taking up the cues the show offers for understanding the role of theatre in the civic culture of towns that are, like Wigan, navigating long-term challenges of industrial decline. *Rent Party*, in its collaborative process, ethic of care, and unruly aesthetic – played its part in the town's civic plan with critical distinction. The term 'civic' is commonly used to refer to the organisations, institutions and events that create and sustain the public culture of a town, including its public realm. Civic organisations, institutions, and events are dedicated to collective good, produce individual and collective obligations, and affective and social networks that generate a sense of allegiance, identity, belonging, and recognition. However, as historian Jose Harris notes, 'civil society', a close relative of the term civic culture, also occupies a historical terrain defined by 'ambiguity and muddle' (Harris, 2003, p. 7). The term's expansive frame of reference stretches from the values, practices and institutions that discipline the populace in accordance with hegemonic norms, through to practices that celebrate individual and collective autonomy. In this chapter, I explore an alternative understanding of the civic, examining how its expansive frame is underpinned by obscured histories of inequity and violence, rooted in legacies of colonialism that, in turn, raise questions about the exclusionary potency of civic culture as a set of practices.

Drawing on *Rent Party* in Wigan, the chapter proposes an egalitarian modality of civic culture – one that centres alterity and otherness, fragility and care, and the unruly and unregulated. The forms of solidarity, identification and recognition that provided sources of inspiration for *Rent Party* travel across space and time, and materialise what feminist scholar Gayatri Gopinath has called a 'queer regional imaginary' (Gopinath, 2018, p. 5). At one and the same time anchored in its locality and dispersed across historical time and geographical space, the show occupies a place inside but also unsettles the limiting frames of civic culture.

Civic regeneration and Wigan town centre

The Old Courts arts centre is situated at one end of Wigan's King Street, formerly the 'nerve centre of the town', due to its proximity to prestigious businesses, high-end residencies and the old town hall (Meehan, n.d.). Walk the length of King Street today, and you will pass two train stations that divide the town centre, with Wigan Pier canal network on one side and the town's civic and retail quarter, including council and leisure services hub, town hall, college, historic arcades, market and indoor shopping complexes, on the other. King Street was a place of civic and commercial function, leisure and entertainment, containing seven theatres and public halls at the height of the town's nineteenth-century expansion. With industrial decline, the street became a place of boarded up shops and half-derelict buildings, interspersed with bars and nightclubs that come alive after dark, and 'widely known for its party-hard, 10 drinks for £10, 11pm to 6am culture' (Old Courts, 2021). The eastern part of the street was designated a High Street Heritage Action Zone in 2018, set to receive £1,271,177 to revive the area as the 'go to' place for townspeople 'to engage in culture and leisure activities' (Historic England, n.d.). In the same year, Wigan Council launched a new cultural strategy, 'The Fire Within' (Al and Al, 2019) and Arts in the Mill CIC – the company that owns The Old Courts – purchased the nineteenth-century Royal Court Theatre, situated at the other end of King Street from the courts, with a commitment to faithfully renovate the building as a theatre and transform it into a community asset. Originally built in 1886, the Royal Court Theatre, after a long life as a theatre, cinema, bingo hall, and nightclub, had stood empty for many years.

The architecture of Wigan town centre exhibits the civic confidence associated with its nineteenth-century prosperity, with impressive albeit neglected buildings offering, as noted in the town centre redevelopment plan, 'clarity of form around the historic centre' (Deloitte, 2019, p. 22). In common with many industrial towns in the UK, Wigan's expansion saw the emergence of a civic infrastructure that provided its increasing population with a framework to foster connection and a shared sense of identity and place. The cultural and social forms produced, from workers' education initiatives, municipal institutions, through to new modes of 'rational recreation', were infused with Victorian ideals of civility, virtue and restraint, self-help and self-improvement (see Bailey, 1978). In their expansive, mid-twentieth-century study of civic culture, social scientists Gabriel Almond and Sidney Verba describe the historical emergence of civic culture in Britain as central to the production of norms, behaviours and virtues that, over time, produce a stable, democratic culture (Almond and Verba, 1963, p. 8). But in his exploration of English towns, historian Peter Borsay notes that 'the concept of the civic ideal is fraught with difficulties', with civic buildings, institutions and an annual calendar of spectacle, ceremony and event helping to manage social conflict and serve altruistic purposes whilst also providing cover for furthering sectional interests and affirming local hierarchies (Borsay, 1990, pp. 35–6). The 'civilising' imperative of civic culture, associated with the production and regulation of English towns and by implication their publics, is also, as Catherine Hall has shown, central to the colonising project of British empire (Hall, 2002). As literature scholar Lisa Lowe has also shown, the 'intimacies' between global conditions of trade, labour and European liberal culture, including for my purposes here, civic culture, are 'deeply implicated in colonialism, slavery, capitalism and empire' (Lowe, 2015, p. 2).

At the time of writing, the 'civic role' of the arts has gained traction as a conceptual ground for the advocacy, recognition and protection of an idea of art and culture as a public good (Gardner, 2019;

Hutton, 2021). In the UK, discourses of civic culture resonate well in a political landscape that embraces cultural factors – including institutions like arts centres and theatres – as part of a 'social infrastructure' (HM Government, 2022, p. 45) providing essential components of the 'complex adaptive systems' that enable places to prosper (ibid., p. 48). A commitment to the concept of civic culture was threaded through the UK government's 'Levelling Up' White Paper (2022), a major policy initiative aiming to address longstanding regional inequalities and productivity gaps across the UK. In the White Paper, a triad of 'people, business and culture' is repeatedly cited as constitutive of thriving urban centres in Western history, from the Italian Renaissance in Florence through to industrial Britain. Here, 'innovation in finance with technological breakthroughs, the cultivation of learning, ground-breaking artistic endeavour, a beautiful built environment and strong civic leadership' provide the ingredients for a 'Medici effect', an idea that describes the prosperity and growth stimulated when 'diverse industries, disciplines and cultures intersect' and there is a 'magnetic attraction of people, culture, commerce and finance' (HM Government, 2022, p. xiv and p. 3; Johansson, 2017).

Advocacy for a civic role for the arts, at best, is driven by a desire to find a place in this terrain that unlocks resource for art and artists, and develops accessible and inclusive modes of making and doing. Civic-minded artistic experiments have, at the time of writing, multiplied in the UK, and there is a sense of renaissance – of new practices responding to old questions about the role of art and culture in living a good life. Underpinning this, there is a desire to revive a post-war social covenant, including a commitment to the idea that 'culture could improve lives, did not need to justify itself and would improve the nation's civic life' (Hutton, 2021, p. 42). The sense of optimism associated with civic culture is inspiring but, I suggest, it also expresses a structure of feeling, prevalent in late capitalist society, identified by cultural theorist Lauren Berlant as 'cruel optimism'. Berlant defines cruel optimism as the affective condition generated when 'postwar optimism for democratic access to the good life' (Berlant, 2011, p. 3) is sustained in the face of a historical present characterised by economic inequality, social precariousness, and sustained crisis that is 'wearing out the power of the good life's traditional fantasy bribe without wearing out the need for a good life' (ibid., p. 7). This is a condition where the life-building projects of the post-war social covenant present a promise whilst also becoming an obstacle: 'optimism is … a scene of negotiated sustenance that makes life bearable as it presents itself ambivalently, unevenly, incoherently' (ibid., p. 14). The promise of renewal in the turn to civic culture, accompanied by investment packages that do not match the amounts stripped from local authority arts budgets over time, feeds a condition of cruel optimism. As towns emerged from the global pandemic of 2020, and as we undertook the research for this book and met communities, public services and a cultural sector exhausted by a sustained period of pressure, the potential for cruel optimistic scenarios seemed all the more acute.

Historian Jose Harris shows how the expansive definition of 'civil society' stretches from understandings of the civic as a means by which market economies become functional, through to civil society as an autonomous zone that mitigates their damaging impact and protects individual freedom (Harris, 2003, pp. 6–7). This ability to morph in response to competing agendas and, in particular, to incorporate both a disciplining *and* emancipatory potency, underpins the enduring appeal of the civic. A less sanguine perspective on this particular morphology of the civic is provided by sociologist Boaventura De Sousa Santos, in his work on epistemic justice. Santos identifies 'abyssal thinking' – 'a system of visible and invisible distinctions' – in forms of thinking associated with Western modernity (Santos, 2014, p. 118). Santos' idea traces a clear line through the fluid terrain of the civic, illuminating its exclusionary potency *and* its inherent instability. For Santos, a 'tension between social regulation and social emancipation' – the same tension that is there in the concept of civic culture – is the 'visible distinction' that underpins Western modernity, repeatedly identifiable across Western forms of metropolitan culture (ibid., p. 118). He asserts, however, that this visible distinction is founded on an *invisible* distinction between metropolitan society and colonial territory, in which 'the colonial is the side of nature where civil society's institutions have no place' (ibid., p. 121). Colonialism – in conceptual and material form – is thus a constitutive, but unacknowledged, part of civil society – reproduced in practices of law, social contract, culture, and values of individuality and free will: 'Western modernity, rather than meaning the abandonment of the state of nature and passage to civil society, means the coexistence of both the civil society and the state of nature, separated by an abyssal line whereby the hegemonic eye, located in civil society, ceases to see' (ibid., p. 122). Following Santos, it becomes possible to situate advocacy of civic culture on a fault-line between, on the one hand, an expression of what 'good' public culture might look like and, on the other, obscuring, ignoring or simply failing to see the systemic harm that discourses and practices of civic culture, past and present, are founded on.

The story of Wigan's town hall is pertinent here. A Grade II listed building, the town hall was originally Wigan Mining College, a civic venture embodying the self-help principles of the Victorian era. The founding of the college in 1857 was financed by public subscription, including substantial contributions from the 24th and 25th Earls of Crawford, James Lindsay and his son, Alexander Lindsay, one of the first families to sink mines in the town and founders of the Wigan Coal and Iron Company (Roderick and Stephens, 1972). James' father was a former Governor of Jamaica (1794–1801) and a slave owner. Following the Slavery Abolition Act (1833) and Slave Compensation Act (1837), the family was awarded a substantial compensation for their slaves. Notably, enslaved people were not awarded compensation following abolition and many transferred into punitive forms of coerced apprenticeship, whilst James Lindsay was 'able to use his family's wealth – derived in significant part from slavery – to invest in the profitable coal industry' (Legacies of British Slavery Database, 2022). A public discussion of legacies of slavery in Wigan was prompted by visits of renowned Jamaican musician, Ripton Lindsay, to his ancestral home in Wigan, the mansion and grounds of Haigh Hall, in 2020 and 2021. Ripton Lindsay had traced his family history to the 23rd Earl of Crawford – the former Governor of Jamaica – his great-great-great-great grandfather. During these visits, Lindsay met council leaders, gave public talks, and served on the judging panel of the inaugural North West Music Awards. He has noted that the dates of Haigh Hall's nineteenth century reconstruction coincided with the award of slave compensation, and yet there is no public record of its relationship to the slave trade (Nowell, 2020). To complete the story, Haigh Hall and its grounds are now part of the civic infrastructure of Wigan, purchased by Wigan Corporation in 1947, open to the public, and currently home to visual artists Al and Al, who led the process of drafting Wigan's cultural manifesto, 'The Fire Within', an important component of Wigan's twenty-first century civic plan. 'The Fire Within' – in its language and visual imagery – makes use of the metaphor of coal, 'the explosive ground beneath our feet', to express the potential of creativity to renew the socioeconomic prospects of the town (Al and Al, 2019, p. 3).

How might civic culture be constructed in a way that, following Ripton Lindsay's lead, fosters awareness of the relationship between towns and historical atrocities, and sustains an open conversation about their legacies? Does the concept of the civic simply need critical framing to 'redefine' or 'reclaim' it – or should it be 'relegated'?[2] A return to Santos' work is useful here. As the short tour of King Street evidences, Wigan has been profoundly challenged by shifts in the global economy created by the emergence of a neoliberal economic framework from the 1970s, which has produced what Santos calls a 'tectonic shake-up of the abyssal global lines' (Santos, 2014, p. 125). Evoking public debates about 'left-behind' towns in the UK, Santos argues that growing insecurity, increased inequality, state withdrawal from social provision and political polarity create a context in which 'workers and popular classes are expelled from the social contract through the elimination of social and economic rights, thereby becoming discardable populations' (Santos, 2014, p. 131). In their research on the Wigan Deal (a local response to a government policy of economic austerity following the financial crash of 2007/8), Chris Naylor and Dan Wellings note that Wigan council was forced to make more than £140 million in cuts and lost around one-fifth of its workforce between 2011 and 2019 (Naylor and Wellings, 2019, p. 5). In the same eight-year period, there was a £413 per person fall in annual council spending across the North of England, with the amount allocated to the region from the UK government's Levelling Up Fund in 2021 equating to £32 per person (Webb et al, 2022, p. 12).

From this perspective, the turn to the civic is taking place in the context of a socioeconomic policy ('Levelling Up') that represents, to cite political scientists, Will Jennings, Lawrence McKay, and Gerry Stoker, a 'political spectacle', providing 'symbols of change' and a 'narrative of success', whilst failing to address longstanding inequalities (Jennings, McKay and Stoker, 2021, p. 302). Wigan is a large town in the devolved city region of Greater Manchester, and in Manchester city centre, a 'Medici effect' of sorts has certainly generated symbols of success, perhaps especially discernable in the growth and reputation of the creative industries in the city. But it has also coincided with high rates of inequality both in the city and in the surrounding towns (Greater Manchester Independent Inequalities Commission, 2021). An economic model that embraces competition produces winners and losers and, as Julian Dobson's analysis of the negative impact of retail-led regeneration in Liverpool city centre on the centres of nearby towns (including Wigan) makes clear, 'in the process of creating a new narrative for one city or town, stories are also written for the places that surround them' (Dobson, 2015, p. 27). That said, a view from theatre and performance studies – the disciplinary framework that underpins this book – supports the alternative argument that symbol, narrative, and spectacle *can* in fact play a critical and powerful role in civic regeneration. If, as political philosopher Michel Feher notes, investment circulates in late capitalism by means of decisions on credit rating, that is, on how those projects that 'deserve to be financed' are selected (Feher, 2018, p. 17), those in need of investment need a good story, and symbol, narrative, and spectacle can help to unlock resource. In this context, artists in towns can help direct how symbol, narrative and spectacle shape a speculation. As Feher argues, the territory of speculation is a potent site of activist intervention, with appropriation of the conditions imposed on those exposed to valuations presenting a route to resist the economic game: 'today's activists will have to inhabit their condition as investees ... the task of a movement of investees is to participate, for its own purposes, in this game of self-fulfilling prophecies. It is, in other words, a question of "counterspeculating"' (Feher, 2018, pp. 57–58).

Rent Party offers a counterspeculation of sorts, asking its audiences to look critically at the manner in which the value of artists, communities and places become legible. The production took place against a backdrop of town centre renewal where a tangible search for an alternative to the economic game of winners and losers was underway, the outcome of which is, at the time of writing, uncertain. The Galleries, a failed retail project bought back into public ownership by the local authority in 2018, is in a process of phased transformation into an entertainment hub, outdoor performance site and apartment complex, led by City Heart property developers and Beijing Construction Engineering Group International (BCEGI), a Chinese state-owned construction company. A mixture of public money and private investment supports the transformation, with the overall cost being £190 million, of which £135 million is allocated to BCEGI as construction partner (Timan, 2021). Local groups have raised questions about ownership of assets, the risk to historic buildings, the fate of the town's marketplace, and the human rights record of the Chinese government. The venture reflects a deliberate policy of attracting Chinese investment by 'Northern Powerhouse' (the UK's economic strategy for devolution in the North of England and Wales). It also reflects the limited economic power of local authorities, where supporting major reconstruction projects deemed essential to the survival of town centres remains a question of brokering partnerships with global players. Here, in a reversal of the road travelled by Orwell, a cash-strapped local authority, in common with many others in the Powerhouse region, decided that 'its fortunes lie with the largesse of a rising China' (Hunt, 2014, p. 413), evidencing the emergence of 'a new imperial landscape' (ibid., p. 416). Changes in political temperature have shifted the playing field since the original agreement and, at the time of writing, parts of the Galleries remain in public ownership, with BCEGI signing up to the local council's 'community wealth building' policy, committing to drawing 60% of labour for the construction from Wigan and the Northwest, and spending £52 million in the local supply chain (Galleries25, n.d.).

'The road from Mandalay to Wigan is a long one and the reasons for taking it are not immediately clear' wrote Orwell, explaining how his concern to learn more about working class life in England was stimulated by his sense of its connections to, and his profound discomfort at, the violence he witnessed as a police officer in colonial Burma (Orwell, 2001[1937], p. 113). George Orwell's great-great-grandfather was a slave owner in Jamaica (as were others in his ancestral line), and his family wealth provided access to the elite education that ensures that his voice was heard and still frames Wigan today. The road travelled by Orwell in his book, infused with socialist commitment but also patrician constructions of people and place, has turned out to be a lengthy one, not yet well worn, and remaining in need of radical deconstruction.

Old Courts, New Deal: A counterspeculation

'If all the world's a stage, then Wigan needs a big one. Yes! The Royal Court' rasps Hacker T. Dog, children's television presenter and dog puppet, born and bred in Wigan. In the short film he introduces, featured on the Royal Court Theatre Facebook page, representatives from Wigan's arts, business and community sector warmly welcome the prospect of having a large-scale theatre 'on our doorstep' that will become 'a vibrant epicentre of theatre, music, dance, comedy and belonging ... giving our local community a stage to shine'. The leader of a local dance studio looks forward to 'the opportunity to showcase my children on stage without having to leave the borough' and the opening of a new theatre is noted as good news for the hospitality sector by a local restaurant owner. The large capacity gives the venture a chance of becoming a viable commercial proposition, as a touring stop for high-profile acts, allowing cross-subsidy for local groups seeking a space for annual galas. The profoundly civic-minded move to purchase the historic building, undertaken by local cultural entrepreneurs with a track record of success – having led the successful renovation of The Old Courts since 2018 – was enabled by drawing on private income gained from work in the commercial entertainment sector. Developments in the renovation are widely reported in the local press and, whilst the work was undertaken, the building itself was wrapped in a specially designed banner, featuring famous performers associated with the town, including Wigan-born popular act George Formby and townspeople in banana and dinosaur costumes, a homage to the popular Wigan tradition of coming into town on Boxing Day in fancy dress.

The Royal Court Theatre and Old Courts renovation is driven by local people with strong connections to the town. Jonny Davenport, Artistic Director of the Old Courts commented in an interview that 'we actually care about the buildings, we're not just looking for some space to do our art in. If that was the case we'd go for some soulless prefab new building, which would be much cheaper' (Davenport, 2021). The purchase of the theatre was in part motivated by fear of losing a potential asset: 'what if someone else sees it, someone from a big conglomerate of theatres around Britain, buys it, and takes food off our plate and every other organisation around Wigan ... what if someone comes in and they don't give a shit about the cultural ecology that already exists' (Davenport, 2021). In the context of struggling town centres, local authorities are embracing the civic role of culture, with theatres and arts centres like The Old Courts seen as potentially able to stimulate night-time economies, provide opportunities for connection, and catalyse economic development by repurposing vacant buildings, providing space and support for entrepreneurship and start-up businesses. Many characteristics of this civic framework for economic renaissance are present at The Old Courts in Wigan, which functions as a hub for social and cultural enterprise, a performance venue, and also – during the pandemic – provided essential social services, including as a food and medical distribution centre for the town. Whilst the combination of civic responsibility, enterprise, pragmatism, collaboration and care that drives all this chimes well with the fraught political terrain of the civic, it is also clear that there are many in Wigan ready to take opportunities to develop the cultural life of the town, in partnership with a range of community groups, professionals and other agencies, and in ways they are scripting for themselves. In the context of a 'meandering abyssal line', to return to Santos' formulation, and – to borrow the words of Wigan's cultural manifesto – '[w]e can expect no one else to do it for us' (Al and Al, 2019, p. 14).

This drive is part of a wider local authority strategy 'The Deal 2030', known locally as the Wigan Deal, which places 'community wealth building' at the heart of the borough. Originally focused on sustaining a safety net in a time of eye-watering budget cuts visited on local authorities by economic austerity, the Wigan Deal has developed into an entire framework for civic governance, centring on a social contract that commits the council to low levels of council tax, culture change in service provision, and partnership working between local authority, businesses and communities, in return for active participation of residents in community life, including in voluntary activities. It explicitly encourages experimentation among its workforce, giving over power to communities and asset-based working (Naylor and Wellings, 2019, p. 5). Geographer Matthew Thompson locates the turn to community wealth building in the UK in the 'New Municipalism' movement that was 'forged desperately in the bonfire of fiscal crises sparked by neoliberal state disciplining of local government' (Thompson, 2021, p. 324).

New Municipalism is a movement of local authorities, activist groups and social networks emerging from the anti-austerity protests following the global financial crash of 2007/8 which were, in turn, inspired by anti-colonial activism across the global South through the twentieth and early twenty-first century. These movements imagine and enact alternatives to the neoliberal economic practices that have dominated global economic policy since the late 1970s, associated with boom-and-bust development, damage to communities created by economic austerity, and growth in economic inequalities. In the UK, community wealth building has been adopted by several local authorities – most famously, by Preston in Lancashire – and it supports economic practices that catalyse local development and keep money invested locally, with anchor institutions committing to progressive procurement and making use of local labour and supply chains. Community wealth building tends to include material support for cooperatives and the social economy, embracing co-production and collaborative working, public ownership and shared decision-making (CLES, 2019, pp. 8–9).

Community wealth building may create space for people-centred development that helps to counter the risk, implicit in the civic realm, of hegemonic, myopic and exclusionary practices. The history of the Wigan Deal is certainly suggestive of this potential. Hilary Cottam's concept of 'radical help' was an important influence on the Deal, outlining a model of relational welfare and a capability-focused public service, building on architect of the Welfare State, William Beveridge's regret that he had designed people power and relationships out of the system (Cottam, 2018, p. 46). Like the civic entrepreneurialism of The Old Courts, locally-scripted initiatives can be imaginative, pragmatic, and responsive to the contingencies of place. In their ethnography of the influential Preston Model, one of the first community wealth building models adopted in the UK, Julian Manley and Philip Whyman describe affective, bottom-up, improvised scripts as crucial to its effectiveness. For Manley and Whyman, the success of the Preston Model is founded on its character as 'an unusual hotpotch of semi-related developments that loosely hang together ... a determination to make the most of whatever can be made to succeed at any given moment and in collaboration with a wide range of local actors' (Manley and Whyman, 2021, p. 9). In Wigan, these loose scripts include citations of discourses of collective action associated with the former industrial landscape, with the introduction to The Deal 2030 including the comment, 'solidarity and working for the common good is in the borough's DNA' (Wigan Council, 2019, p. 8).

Many artists and practitioners working across the cultural sector have historically participated in forms of community wealth building, in their commitment to principles of collaboration and equity, and working practices that centre the capacity, imagination and potential of people and place. The Old Courts' participation in the Moving Roots co-creation model firmly locates the organisation inside this history. Co-creation is a creative methodology and way of organising cultural projects that responds to widespread recognition that, after decades of outreach and 'targeting' by formal cultural institutions failing to redistribute resource in the cultural sector, a new model is needed (Tiller, 2017, p. 11). Privileging collaboration, co-design and partnership from the inception of projects, co-creation commits to generative rather than extractive or transactional relationship with communities (Heart of Glass and BAC 2021, p. 22). In the UK, the Battersea Arts Centre (BAC) in London has worked over time to build an approach to co-creation that moves beyond 'a narrow model of participation (to come and join in) towards a model of co-creation (to come and create)' (Jubb, 2017). Moving Roots is a co-created touring programme administered by BAC and led by cultural partners in England and Wales in areas underserved by arts funding, and it focuses on a performance work or project that is reimagined via a process of co-creation at each stop of the touring network. *Rent Party* was selected as the first of three co-created pieces taking place over the funded period. Performed in each venue through 2021, the *Rent Party* shows were supported by 'Sounding Boards', made up of local people carefully recruited and paid to shape, direct and develop Moving Roots in a way that addresses the needs, priorities, and concerns of each distinct locality. The aim was to move from a top-down model of touring that brings work to communities, and towards a locally responsive model that enriches the cultural ecology of a place.

For Darren Pritchard, co-creator and director of *Rent Party*, co-creation – rather than being a radically new approach – represents traditions of working class cultural practice that have been ignored and marginalised in the UK cultural sector: 'as a working class artist you're co-creating all the time because you've never got enough money to do it by yourself' (Pritchard, 2021). Pritchard's point draws attention to the ways in which the cultural sector has reproduced socioeconomic inequalities, in part through inadequate access to training, investment and insecure payment structures that systematically favour artists with private means of supporting themselves. Commenting on *Rent Party*, Pritchard stated, 'I wanted to work with professional performers and with exceptional working class talent that had been overlooked'. For him, what is most important about the co-creation process is that it devolves a large proportion of the budget, unusually for touring shows, to rehearsal time with local performers and producers, who develop important relationships with each other and their own venues – 'we built a working class nepotistic network' (Pritchard, 2021). That every *Rent Party* show in each venue sold out evidences the unsurprising fact that it is perfectly possible to create an alternative cultural infrastructure – one based on sharing rather than hoarding, and founded on the wealth of diverse talent in areas neglected by arts funders.

Queering the civic spectacle: *Rent Party* in Wigan

Towards the end of *Rent Party*, as the party begins to wind down, we are introduced to Shaun Fallows, a poet familiar on the spoken word scene in Wigan. Dressed in a smart black jacket and winkle-picker boots, his wheelchair gleaming in the spotlight, Shaun tells a story of a formative moment in his journey to becoming an artist, when he was 16 years old and at residential college in Cheltenham. 'I love talking but I wasn't always like that. I used to be very quiet and happy to let people do stuff for me', he says. 'At certain points in your life though, there are catalysts for change. And mine was a guy called Derrick'. Derrick had limited mobility and 'he couldn't speak':

> I wanted to help Derrick in some tiny way, so I taught him a new word. The staff would come in and say "Where's he got that from?" I'd say "It's probably TV" – but it was me. I taught him to say "Fuck off". And I'm proud that he had some small way to stick up for himself …
>
> When I saw how the staff reacted to Derrick, I was so scared that it would happen to me. From that day I said "I want more, I have to do more".

Shaun then performs his poem, 'What they said to Derrick', with one particular lyric, repeated twice:

> "What will we do with you Derrick?" was what they always said.
> And what they always did with Derrick, was put Derrick to bed.

Shaun's story of teaching a peer to perform a gesture of incivility is the show's powerful final act. A poet from Wigan teaches cast and audience how they might respond to those who would dismiss, ignore, marginalise or fail to see them – a valuable life lesson. Up to this point, we had witnessed a succession of performances accompanied by personal stories of effort – to fit in, adapt, come out, access opportunity, develop, compromise, fulfil promise, control thoughts and feelings, find secure locations from which to self-represent, try to measure up, love, work, to matter. Each performance showcased working class performers from the town, who, whilst paid a full salary for their work on *Rent Party*, were not yet earning a secure living from their artistic talent, making a living from care, education or retail jobs or receiving state support to cover living costs, with intermittent earnings from gigs and involvement in arts projects. The performance contained autobiographical stories of struggle and celebration, carefully balanced between presenting difficulty and works-in-progress of overcoming sometimes everyday, sometimes life-defining, moments of challenge. Shaun's lesson in incivility was a wickedly funny, sharp rebuke to a context that demands such sustained effort whilst also limiting opportunity. It came at the end of a show that offered a powerful prefiguration of an alternative way of doing culture – critical, connected, diverse, humane, full of feeling, imaginative, celebratory, lyrical, and inspiring, here and now, in an old courtroom in Wigan.

Figure 3.1 The cast at The Old Courts. From left to right – Yasmin Goulden, Zha Olu, Darren Pritchard, Jamie Lee, Shaun Fallows, Stuart Bowden, Sarah Hardman, Alice Mae Fairhurst. Photographer, Ant Robling

Wigan has a reputation as a music town, so it was not surprising that the Wigan *Rent Party* had the atmosphere of a live music gig, but the talent on show was not drawn from the male, working class and white 'indie' bands typically identified with the town. The collectively written Moving Roots Manifesto expressed a commitment to 'dig deeper', and this involved an unconventional casting process. At The Old Courts, whilst there was an open call, producer Jess O'Neill connected with performers beyond 'the usual suspects' confident and experienced enough to attend a formal audition, and the auditions themselves took the form of a jam night combined with an informal workshop (O'Neill, 2021). For The Old Courts, the hope was that this would encourage the cast to potentially 'change their perceptions of themselves and the value they have' not just through the showcase provided, but also through the opportunity to perform their story (O'Neill, 2021). In the words of one performer, Sarah Hardman, *Rent Party* showed that 'we're not just there to sing and entertain, there's more to us' (Hardman, 2021). With three female singer-songwriters, Alice Fairhurst, Sarah Hardman, and Zha Olu in the Wigan cast, Pritchard 'wanted a moment for women to just take that space and sing a love song', and this happened early in the show, providing the moment when the show 'went full Wigan' (Pritchard, 2022). Following Zha Olu's monologue, in which she tells the story of coming out to her Nigerian heritage, Christian family, the three singer-songwriters came together to sing a love song, US rhythm and blues classic 'Tennessee Whiskey'. As well as being quintessentially Wigan, this moment materialised the Black and queer aesthetic of the original *Rent Party* commission (also present in each of the co-created productions), with the song choice, rooted in rhythm and blues music, sharing a Black heritage with the Harlem rent parties, and also carrying an association with Wigan as a historic centre of Northern Soul. The original arrangement of 'Tennessee Whiskey' in the Wigan *Rent Party* was frequently cited as a powerful moment in the show by the cast and production team. All three female singer-songwriters commented in interviews on their struggles in a local music scene dominated by venue managers that favour male artists, and their shared delight at having a rare opportunity to perform as female musicians together at a live venue in Wigan was tangible: 'when me, Alice and Sarah sang that song together, there was a real connection between us … we were like a force to be reckoned with' (Olu, 2021).

The personal stories shared during the performance produced moments that were moving, down to earth and often humorous. As performance poet Jamie Lee commented, 'in each individual story there's something that I strongly connected to', with Zha Olu emphasising a renewed sense of connection to place as an outcome of the co-production, 'I definitely felt a sense of being proud to live, or work, or be from this area'. Many of the cast reported moments of empathy, familiarity and connection between the distinct struggles shared through the process. Pritchard described the importance of the ethic of care in the structure of the show and embedded in rehearsal room culture, created by the producers in each locality, as well as by Stuart Bowden, the assistant director and host of each *Rent Party* – the previously mentioned 'Queen of this court', and an established dancer and choreographer in his own right. Bowden was crucial to establishing a practice of care in rehearsals and performances, and throughout the co-created tour, local producers went the extra mile, from organising lifts to and from the train station, to being embedded in the rehearsal room with the creative team. This additional infrastructure of care and support was important. As Pritchard commented 'because of the people I wanted in the show it all became about the care of those people and the experience that they had … we had to create our own little world in the system and it worked' (Pritchard, 2022).

Darren Pritchard, a professional dancer and choreographer who identifies as queer, working class and Black, has had a long career as a maker of experimental theatre and dance, and is prominent in the vogue scene in the North of England, a vibrant queer performance network inspired by the drag balls of 1980s New York (Watson and Keighron-Foster, 2018). Prior to *Rent Party*, Pritchard was well known in the theatre sector for a collaboration between his dance company, Company Fierce, and performance company, Quarantine, leading to the celebrated show, *Susan and Darren*, which Darren performed with his mother, Susan. This deeply moving piece has toured internationally since 2006, with the performance space, narratively mapped by the performers at the beginning of the show, creating a visceral sense of being welcomed as party guests in Susan and Darren's home in Hulme in central Manchester (with some audience members enlisted into making sandwiches and cheese and pineapple sticks for the guests). An aesthetic of personal story, direct address, Afro-Caribbean celebration (a feature of Pritchard's upbringing), and the warmth, humour and candour of a working class welcome of *Susan and Darren* were all present in *Rent Party*. Pritchard had come across rent parties when researching Langston Hughes, a Black American poet and writer, believed to be gay, and commonly cited as the voice of the Harlem Renaissance. Rent parties are described by Langston Hughes as convivial gatherings of residents of Black working class Harlem that took place 'not always to pay the rent' but also to have a 'get-together of

Figure 3.2 Shaun Fallows – *Rent Party*, Wigan. Photographer, Ant Robling

one's own' without risk of being 'stared at by white folks' frequenting Harlem clubs (Hughes, 1993[1940], pp. 228–229). Hughes' contemporary, poet and playwright Wallace Thurman, described rent parties as gatherings that served 'a real and vital purpose', providing a source of revenue but also a place of enjoyment, assembly and relief for Black communities (Thurman in Singh and Scott, 2003, p. 54).

Rent Party created multi-directional flows between different sites of Black and queer culture in ways that stretched across time and space – from the rent parties of 1920s Harlem to the Afro-Caribbean parties and drag balls of twenty-first-century Northwest England – which hark back to the vogue dance scene of 1980s New York, that, in turn, looked to the lindy hop and blues and soul of the Harlem Renaissance. The latter provided inspiration for the soul music of mid-America as well as carried forms, gestures, and notes across the complex geographies and histories of Black cultural expression, and – forward in time and across place – to the Northern Soul dance and music scene of the midlands and North of England in the 1970 and 80s. As noted in the introduction, these multi-directional flows, gathered together in the Black and queer aesthetic of *Rent Party*, evoke what Gayatri Gopinath calls a 'queer regional imaginary', an idea that maps cultural production as a relational field that intersects with legacies of colonialism. This concept supports an understanding of *Rent Party*, and its broader contexts of production, as a civic form of artistic expression that counters abyssal lines by traversing between and connecting colonial pasts and presents. Gopinath argues that the aesthetic practices of queer diaspora:

> allow us to see, sense, and feel the promiscuous intimacies of multiple times and spaces. They bring into the realm of a "violent present", glimpses of past desires, longings, and articulations of alternative social and political worlds that provide the occasion for a different sense of possibility and horizon.
>
> (Gopinath, 2018, p. 18)

Rent Party maps well onto Gopinath's rubric of a queer regional imaginary, connecting intersectional and marginalised artists in ways that bypass formal networks of metropolitan culture, and trace 'lines of queer affiliation across disparate locations' (Gopinath, 2018, p. 169). In the process, *Rent Party*'s queer regional imaginary allowed it to counter an imaginary of Wigan as dominated by industrial labour and landscapes of poverty, replacing these with a projection of diverse artistic, creative, and cultural work-in-progress of artists deeply connected to the town. In place of scenarios of industrialisation and poverty, we encounter a group of working class, queer, Black and differently-abled performers, engage in a new speculation on how art and culture might contribute to living a good life in this town, and at the same time affirm a significant cultural institution, The Old Courts, as an anti-racist, feminist, accessible and queer-friendly civic space. That said, it is important to note that concerns about the accessibility of The Old Courts to wheelchair users have been vocalised locally, with Shaun Fallows commenting that he struggled with access during the rehearsal and performance period: 'it's probably the best in Wigan but it's still not right' (Fallows, 2021).

There are relations of power in the 'promiscuous intimacies' of time and place denoted by a queer regional imaginary. In Wigan, these manifest in several ways, including in the town's association with soul music, which filters through the performance of *Rent Party*. Wigan was a centre of the 1970s and 80s Northern Soul dance and music movement, which inspired the identification of a generation of young, majority white, working class people growing up in towns beginning to experience startling levels of decline in the North and midlands, with the Soul music of mid-twentieth-century America. Shaun

Fallows, describing himself as 'obsessed with soul music', comments on the power of this identification:

> I love the music, but more than anything it was the fact that, for me as well, those guys like Ray Charles and all those people, they didn't have anything but they were really sharp, you know. We don't have anything but we can look really good. We don't have anything but we can still enjoy the things we do. I feel really akin to what they were trying to do even though it was a different issue of race.

There is an important debate about Northern Soul as an appropriation and fetishisation of Black culture, from the 'penny capitalism' of white entrepreneurs buying up soul music (with no royalties for Black artists) through to the use of the Black Power symbol by the Wigan Casino, a now demolished Northern Soul venue in Wigan's town centre. Northern Soul provided a 'soundtrack' for a time of uncertainty and a form of positive cross-racial identification, whilst 'operating outside of the wider struggle for racial equality' (Catterall and Gildart, 2020, p. 221). Similarly important is the debate on the extent to which a white audience is able to fully appreciate a cultural form embedded in Black experience (Rudinow, 1994). That said, Shaun's love for the work of a prominent Black musician, who was himself disabled, is a positive identification, not least because it is embedded in an acknowledgement of difference ('it was a different issue of race'). I would also counter a simplistic equation of commercial exploitation of Black culture with the penny capitalism of Northern Soul. In his history of Northern Soul, David Nowell describes how newly available cheap flights allowed Wigan promoters to travel to warehouses in the US containing masses of discarded soul records that had failed in the US market, buying in bulk at cut prices and selling in the UK, providing a new market relevance for overlooked Soul singers (Nowell, 2015, pp. 138–139). Here, an informal, low value economy – typical of working class towns – created a social and cultural phenomena founded on revaluing the outputs of talented Black musicians. These circulations of identification and value, whilst not resolving longstanding racial injustices, hold open the possibility of positive kinds of association, identification and relationship, founded on respect for difference. Pritchard's identification with Harlem rent parties, working a little differently, was inspired by a profound sense of recognition. The long-term neglect of Black British culture in the UK mainstream meant that, as a Black artist, New York became his 'go-to culture … if I was living in the

1920s, I would have been throwing a rent party ... I just see myself, but with a different accent' (Pritchard, 2022).

Rent Party provided a counter-speculation on the potential of civic culture in towns. It rented a critical corner in civic space and, occupying this, brought artists together to experiment, share stories, make a play, and have a party. In queering practices of institutional culture in its form, content, and touring practice, and in ways that sensitively and critically interacted with local performance networks, *Rent Party* locates an alternative performance culture at the centre of civic life. The play itself was central to the success of this critical move. It encouraged the performers to play the condition of investee asking for money in return for displays of talent, interrupting with playful irony the conditions in which their artistic talent, and a town's creative economy, is allocated credit. *Rent Party* also drew energy from the unruly aesthetic of the party form. This was especially present in its song choices, from Aloe Blacc's 'I need a dollar', with its lyric that promises to share a story of desperation in return for money, to 'Dirty Cash', with its references to using the body for sexual and financial reward. There is cruelty and humour here, with the stories, games and songs performed within a framework of shared, common experience – a register set up in the opening of the show, with the host's description of the audience as 'the great unwashed ... you know what I'm talking about'. Economic austerity is a point of critique throughout, often provided via moments of direct address or audience participation. A party game of 'pass the parcel' takes place that is impossible to win, as 'budget cuts' mean that there was only one wrapping and the prize inside the parcel was not a prize and rather an imaginary Wigan kebab (Wigan is known for the unique nature of its kebabs-buttered barm cakes with a meat pie in the middle).

This chapter has presented an example of the positive role played by civic spectacles in towns, with an emphasis on the inter- and intra-regional and intersectional modalities of civic expression exemplified by *Rent Party* and the Moving Roots co-created touring practice. The context of production, The Old Courts – based in a renovated municipal building and led by an arts enterprise that, at the time of writing, is in the process of transforming a derelict nineteenth-century theatre into a community-oriented, commercially viable venue – provides an imaginative, critical, and pragmatic projection of civic culture. Maybe such civic spectacles, founded on intimacies and solidarities across time and place, are more likely to happen in towns than cities. Imagining connections between this place and time and other times and places has always been theatre's gift, and in towns, perhaps these connections are easier to trace or more difficult to ignore. Here, the relationship between cultural spaces, and discourses and practices of civic culture and socio-economic development, can be held up to view, reshaped and unsettled.

Rent Party draws indirect attention to longer histories of complicity between civic culture and systemic economic inequality and violence which, like many towns across the region (and the nation it is part of), was an agent and beneficiary of the slave economy, in ways that urgently need to be addressed in the regional and national story. *Rent Party* transplanted a performance economy created by the generations of Black Americans directly impacted by slavery to a post-industrial town in the North of England. It connected people and culture across time and place, and invited those who experience themselves as out of place to a party – providing a counter-speculation on the civic value of theatre, and one that countered the civilising impulses of self-improvement associated with historic civic traditions. It consciously and deliberately fails to fit in with metropolitan cultural norms. I hope that the analysis in the chapter has begun the work of addressing the abyssal lines implicit in traditions of civic thought, and their historical influence on performance practices. At best, a radical civic culture is materialised – one that centres alterity and intersectionality, counters ableism, and allows diverse shapes of what it means to be an artist, a theatre, and a town to be prefigured. *Rent Party*, and the model of co-created touring it was part of, suggests an alternative civic culture – one that celebrates the ways that theatres in towns are part of, and mobilise, diverse and distributed local, regional, national, and global cultural imaginaries and material networks. It asks, not only how to provide stages to nurture, platform and celebrate talent and support good life in this place, but also, when to refuse, forge an alternative path and change the rules of the game.

Notes

1 The original *Rent Party* was commissioned by Homotopia, an arts and social justice organistion dedicated to platforming work by LGBTQIA artists. The collective of organisations making up Moving Roots at the time of the show were Battersea Arts Centre, Common Wealth, Jumped Up Theatre, Lyrici Arts, and The Old Courts. Moving Roots was funded by the Esmée Fairbairn Foundation and the Garfield Weston Foundation.
2 Credit for this form of words belongs to Tribe Arts, the collaborating organisation on the 'Civic Theatres: A Place for Towns' AHRC-funded project. As part of the research, Tribe Arts conceived, designed and

facilitated an original version of their innovative 'Tribe Talks': 'Decolonising the Civic: Reclaim, Redefine or Relegate?' This event took place on 6 October 2021.

References

Al and Al. (2019). The Fire Within. Wigan: Wigan Council.
Almond, G.A. and Verba, S. (1963). *The Civic Culture: Political Attitudes in Five Nations*. USA: Princeton University Press.
Armstrong, S. (2012). *The Road to Wigan Pier Revisited*. London: Constable.
Bailey, P. (1978). *Leisure and Class in Victorian England: Rational Recreation and the Contest for Control, 1830–1885*. London: Routledge.
Berlant, L. (2011). *Cruel Optimism*. Durham & London: Duke University Press.
Borsay, P. (eds.) (1990). *The Eighteenth Century Town: A Reader in English Urban History 1688–1820*. London & New York: Longman.
Campbell, B. (1984). *Wigan Pier Revisited*. London: Virago.
Catterall, S. and Gildart, K. (2020). 'Race, Gender, Sexuality and the Politics of Northern Soul'. In Catterall S. & Gildart, K. (eds.), *Keeping the Faith: A History of Northern Soul*. Manchester: Manchester University Press.
CLES. (2019). 'How we built community wealth in Preston'. Centre for Local Economic Strategies.
Cottam, H. (2018). *Radical Help: How We can Remake the Relationships between Us and Revolutionise the Welfare State*. London: Virago.
Davenport, J. (2021). Interview with the author. Wigan.
Deloitte LPP, on behalf of Wigan Borough Council. (2019). 'Wigan Town Centre Strategic Regeneration Framework.' Available at: https://www.wigan.gov.uk/Docs/PDF/Business/Economic-vision/Wigan-Town-Centre-Strategic-Regeneration-Framework-2019.pdf [Accessed 23 June 2022].
Dobson, J. (2015). *How to Save Our Town Centres: A Radical Agenda for the Future of High Streets*. Bristol: Policy Press.
Fallows, S. (2021). Interview with the author. Wigan and Manchester.
Feher, M. (2018). *Rated Agency: Investee Politics in a Speculative Age*. New York: Zone Books.
Galleries25. Available at: https://galleries25.com/faqs/ [Accessed 23 June 2022].
Gardner, L. (eds.) (2019) 'What would Joan Littlewood say?' Calouste Gulbenkian Foundation (UK Branch).
Gopinath, G. (2018). *Unruly Visions: The Aesthetic Practices of Queer Diaspora*. Durham & London: Duke University Press.
Greater Manchester Independent Inequalities Commission. (2021). 'The Next Level – Good Lives for All in Greater Manchester'. Available at: https://www.greatermanchester-ca.gov.uk/what-we-do/equalities/independent-inequalities-commission/ [Accessed 2 June 2022].
Hall, C. (2002). *Civilising Subjects: Metropole and Colony in the English Imagination 1830–1867*. Great Britain: Polity Press.
Hardman, S. (2021). Interview with the author. Wigan.

Harris, J. (eds.) (2003). *Civil Society in British History: Ideas, Identities, Formations.* Oxford: Oxford University Press.

Heart of Glass and Battersea Arts Centre. (2021). 'Considering Co-Creation' Available at: https://www.artscouncil.org.uk/sites/default/files/download-file/ConsideringCo-Creation_1.pdf [Accessed 23 June 2022].

Historic England. King Street, Wigan High Street Heritage Action Zone. Available at: https://historicengland.org.uk/services-skills/heritage-action-zones/wigan/ [Accessed 23 June 2022].

HM Government. (2022). 'Levelling Up the United Kingdom'. Crown Copyright.

Hughes, L. (1993 [1940]). *The Big Sea.* New York: Hill & Wang.

Hunt, T. (2014). *Cities of Empire: The British Colonies and the Creation of the Urban World.* New York: Metropolitan Books.

Hutton, D. (2021). *Towards a Civic Theatre.* Bristol: Salamander Street Books.

Jennings, W, McKay, L and Stoker, G. (2021). 'The Politics of Levelling Up,' *The Political Quarterly*, 92(2), pp. 302–311.

Johansson, F. (2017). *The Medici Effect: What Elephants and Epidemics can Teach Us About Innovation.* Boston, Massachusetts: HBR Press.

Jubb, D. (2017). 'Cultural centres need to be led by the passions, interests and concerns of the communities they serve' Available at: https://davidjubb.blog/2019/09/02/how-can-cultural-centres-also-be-community-centres/ [Accessed 23 June 2022].

Legacies of British Slavery Database. (2022) 'James Lindsay, 7th Earl of Balcarres'. Available at: http://wwwdepts-live.ucl.ac.uk/lbs/person/view/21571 [Accessed 2 June 2022].

Lowe, L. (2015). *The Intimacies of Four Continents.* Durham & London: Duke University Press.

Manley, J and Whyman, P.B. (eds.) (2021). *The Preston Model: Creating a Socio-Economic Democracy for the Future.* London & New York: Routledge.

Meehan, J. n.d. 'The Street that Was'. Wigan Local History and Heritage Society. Available at: https://www.wiganlocalhistory.org/king-street-heritage-action-zone/introduction-to-the-street-that-was [Accessed 23 June 2022].

Naylor, C and Wellings, D. (2019). *'A Citizen-Led Approach to Health and Care: Lessons from the Wigan Deal'.* London: The Kings Fund.

Nowell, A. (2020) 'Time for Memorial Recognising Wigan landmark's Links to Slave trade' *Wigan Today.* Available at:https://www.wigantoday.net/news/people/time-memorial-recognising-wigan-landmarks-links-slave-trade-2886452 [Accessed 2 June 2022].

Nowell, D. (2015). *The Story of Northern Soul: A Definitive History of the Dance Scene That Refuses to Die.* London: Pavilion Books.

O'Neill, J. (2021). Interview with the author. Wigan.

Old Courts. (2021). 'Streets Apart Artist Brief'.

Olu, Z. (2021). Interview with the author. Wigan.

Orwell, G. (2001 [1937]). *The Road to Wigan Pier.* London: Penguin.

Pritchard, D. (2021). 'Co-creating change festival 2021'. Battersea Arts Centre.

Pritchard, D. (2022). Interview with the author. Manchester.

Roderick, G.W. and Stephens, M.D. (1972). 'Mining Education in England and Wales in the Second Half of the Nineteenth century', *The Irish Journal of Education*, 6(2), pp. 105–120.

Rudinow, J. (1994). 'Race, Ethnicity, Expressive Authenticity: Can White People Sing the Blues?' *The Journal of Aesthetics and Art Criticism*, 52(1), pp. 27–137.

Santos, B. (2014). *Epistemologies of the Global South: Justice Against Epistemicide*. London & New York: Routledge.

Singh, A and Scott, D.M. (eds.) (2003). *The Collected Writings of Wallace Thurman*. New Brunswick, New Jersey & London: Rutgers University Press.

Thompson, M. (2021). 'What's So New About New Municipalism?' *Progress in Human Geography*, 45(2), pp. 317–342.

Tiller, C. (2017). 'Power Up'. Creative People and Places. Available at: https://www.artscouncil.org.uk/sites/default/files/download-file/Power_Up_think_piece_Chrissie_Tiller__0.pdf [Accessed 23 June 2022].

Timan, J. 'A town torn apart about its future' *Manchester Evening News* 28 December 2021. Available at: https://www.manchestereveningnews.co.uk/news/greater-manchester-news/wigan-town-centre-transform-2022-22569495 [Accessed 2 June 2022].

Watson, A and Keighron-Foster, D. (2018). Deep in Vogue. BBC Documentary.

Webb, J, Johns, M, Roscoe, E, Giovannini, A, Qureshi, A and Baldini, R. (2022). 'State of the North 2021/22: Powering Northern Excellence'. Institute for Public Policy Research North.

Wigan Council. (2019). The Deal 2030. Available at: https://www.wigan.gov.uk/Docs/PDF/Council/The-Deal/Deal-2030.pdf [Accessed 23 June 2022].

4 Volunteer-Led Theatres
Meshworks of a Coastal Town

Cara Gray

Nestled between the East and West Hills of Hastings, a town in East Sussex on the south coast of England, sits the Stables Theatre. Everyone who works there – serving drinks behind the bar, selling tickets at the box office, greeting people at the front of house, scheduling performances, running its archive, maintaining the garden, or taking part in one of its many amateur productions (performing, designing, constructing sets, lighting, sound design and operation, stage management, sourcing props and making costumes) is a volunteer. 'No one is paid' explained Neil Sellman, current Chair of the Stables, 'apart from the cleaner'.[1]

Theatre in towns is often kept alive by volunteers. In the arts, increased cuts leading to increased competition for available funding means that volunteers play a vital role in keeping many arts and cultural institutions and events running. Museums and galleries across the country rely heavily on volunteers to assist in their day-to-day running. Similarly in theatres, front-of-house duties including ushering, selling programmes and checking tickets are frequently undertaken by volunteers whose contribution of time and commitment saves organisations money in exchange for tangible (discounted/free tickets) and intangible (social, skills) benefits (Bussell and Forbes, 2006). Theatres often work on models that see volunteers working alongside and supporting paid members of staff. However, many theatres across England – including the Stables and the Corn Exchange, discussed in Helen Nicholson's chapter – are completely owned, managed, and run by amateur theatre companies. The Little Theatre Guild – an umbrella organisation that assists with the development of amateur theatre companies who own or lease their own theatres – has over 100 active members across the UK and beyond, including both the Stables and the Corn Exchange. Meanwhile, the recent 'amateur turn' within contemporary theatre studies has highlighted the work and enthusiasms of unpaid theatre-makers and their theatres (Nicholson, Holdsworth and Milling, 2018).

DOI: 10.4324/9781003308058-4

This chapter builds upon this work by exploring the role of volunteer theatres in towns by focusing on the Stables Theatre, which holds an important place in the cultural life of Hastings. I use the idea of 'meshworks' as a tool to think this through. Meshwork is a word used by anthropologist Tim Ingold as a metaphor for how life is lived along entangled lines of becoming – emergent, unfixed, and unexpected. Ingold borrows the word from the philosopher Henri Lefebvre, who used meshwork to explain the patterns left by animals and humans as they move around their immediate environments, namely how the 'movements and rhythms of human and non-human activity are registered in lived space' (Ingold, 2010, p. 11). For Ingold, meshworks can be understood by imagining the movements and trails of a wayfarer who walks this way and that, sometimes pausing before moving on and often changing course but is always 'on the way to somewhere else' (Ingold, 2016, p. 83). Over time, these multiple trails, made up of open-ended lines, become interwoven with other trails. Through the wayfarers' multiple movements, they cross over and pass through each other. They tangle and knot but never infinitely connect as they have no end or beginning points. 'It is the entanglement of lines', rather than the 'intersecting routes' of a network, that make the meshwork (Ingold, 2016, p. 83). And it is along these lines of the meshwork that life is lived.

Theatres can be understood as existing in, being sustained by and constantly becoming entangled with the meshwork of their towns. This chapter explores this by placing the Stables within wider discussions around Hastings and English coastal towns – of seasonal rhythms, cultural, and arts led regeneration and the complex landscape of volunteering: including themes of care, creativity, and community ownership – before following the threads back into the theatre. Here, I draw on conversations with volunteers involved in the day to day running of the Stables Theatre, those involved in making the theatre's amateur productions, as well as local theatre-makers who are beginning to use the Stables as a space to perform, rehearse, and workshop. Taken together, the chapter illuminates how wider meshworks have encouraged a hybrid model of theatre and theatre-making to emerge in Hastings, where amateurs, volunteers, and professionals are sharing space but also working together in different ways.

The changing rhythms of coastal towns

My first visit to Hastings was during the summer months of 2021 when the seafront was bustling – loud with the sound of families running in and out of the arcades; taking photographs outside of the Fisherman's

Museum where Hastings' iconic net huts stand – once used to dry fishing nets to save them from rotting; or queuing for doughnuts, candy floss, and ice cream. As autumn approached and then winter, the seafront became quieter, the light became lower, and the crazy golf shut along with the fairground. On one visit, lines of fencing had been put up in front of an ice cream stall. A handful of people, hoods shielding them from the rain, slowly wandered outside the many fish and chip shops along the front, deciding which one to pick. The arcades – still open but empty – created haunting illusions of big wins, as sounds of money cashing out and celebratory flashing lights played on a loop. Along the promenade I passed a few cyclists and some runners. One lone figure stood on the pebbled beach – backlit by the low sun, making them look like a statue. I walked onto the pier (Figure 4.1) – an expanse of empty decking where a couple of seagulls hovered and landed – and looked back at Hastings on my right and St. Leonards on my left. I was able to take in the whole stretch of the town and at that moment was reminded of what numerous members of the Stables

Figure 4.1 Hastings Pier. Photographer: Cara Gray

Theatre had pointed out to me – we lose half of our potential audience because half of the town is the sea.

Experiencing a town changing through the seasons is something felt in many towns on the coast, particularly those with a tourist season. Growing up in Hayle, a coastal town in West Cornwall, the measure of the year would be how long it would take to drive through the town or how many people were queued up outside of the pasty shop. In the winter months, seasonal jobs would wind down in hours or come to an end altogether. The town quietened as tourists and visitors emptied from the beaches and the holiday parks, while some residents left to go back to university, travel or find work elsewhere. Holiday homes sat dormant. These familiar rhythms of life in coastal towns can be understood as being guided or even governed by what Lefebvre calls 'cyclical repetitions' (Lefebvre, 1992). Much like the tides that roll in and out as high tide moves to low tide, twice a day – cyclical repetitions see spring fold into summer, summer into autumn, autumn into winter and so on.

However, these seasonally governed rhythms are increasingly becoming entangled with, and disrupted by, the bigger narratives of change that surround towns on the coast. There are growing calls for coastal towns in England to reinvent and reimagine themselves in order to survive precarious futures. Strategies to attract middle-class, high-spend visitors, extend tourist seasons, and increase day visitors are highlighted in Tim Edensor & Steve Millington's research on Blackpool and its illuminations (Edensor & Millington, 2013). Meanwhile, a recent report by The House of Lords Select Committee, *The future of seaside towns* (2019), builds upon recommendations for culture-led coastal regeneration – proposing that the arts and creative industries have a clear role in supporting seaside reinventions by diversifying their economies. In this section, I follow the threads of arts and culture-led regeneration that weave throughout Hastings; opening up questions around the role of theatre, particularly those that are voluntary run and/or amateur, within towns branding themselves as 'creative'.

'Hastings is going through a period of change'

When I began researching Hastings, the narrative of change surrounded the town. 'Hastings is going through a period of change', writes Historic England who are (at the time of writing) supporting a 'High Street Heritage Action Zone' in the Trinity Triangle area of the town. Meanwhile in June 2021, Hastings was awarded £24.3 million for the Hastings Town Deal with a vision to regenerate the town and increase visitor numbers. However, Hastings can be understood as 'going through a period of change' for a while now. Nestled in amongst the shingle, fishing boats and huts selling fresh fish from hatches, sits a cuboid of black glazed tiles. Once called the Jerwood Gallery, the Hastings Contemporary is an art gallery that sits on the historic Stade – an old Saxon word for 'landing place', as the beach has long been used for launching boats. Built on the site of the old coach station, the £4 million project received some local resistance in the lead up to its opening. 'NO TO JERWOOD' signs dotted around the town and the *Observer* reported how the Hastings Bonfire Society constructed a model of the proposed gallery to set alight during the annual Hastings Bonfire: 'this is just another in a string of things that people are trying to foist on us,' the society's honorary president is reported to have said (Day, 2008).

The opening of the gallery in 2012 seemed to act as a catalyst for 'change' in Hastings. Following its opening, an increasing number of blog posts, Sunday supplements, and lifestyle magazines began to recommend Hastings as an ideal weekend getaway, day trip from London or place to move. Suggestions on where to buy, stay, eat, drink, shop, and what to see and do often cite the gallery as a key attraction. The *Guardian*'s 'Let's move to…' series signalled Hastings, particularly the Old Town, as a best-kept secret ready to be shared with the world – citing 'affordable housing' (relative to London and the South East), the independent shops and cinema, the fish, the pubs, the community spirit and the newly opened Jerwood Gallery (Dyckhoff, 2012). Later, 'An Insider's Guide to Hastings' by *Condé Nast Traveller* described Hastings as the result of a 'perfect storm' of buckets, spades, candyfloss, crazy golf and newly opened spaces by artists, designers, and musicians – including the Jerwood Gallery, 'settling down after a tricky start' (Campbell, 2015).

This juxtaposition of enduring seaside nostalgia mixed with the burgeoning art scene became a recurring theme in following reflection pieces about the town. In 2016, *i-D* called Hastings 'the British creative paradise you haven't heard of', describing it as 'changing and changing fast' while managing to 'walk a tightrope between urban decay and creative rebirth' (Oppenheim, 2016). An appealing combination to the young photographers, filmmakers and animators interviewed who had relocated from London. In the same year, the *Guardian* reflected how 'nearly 950 years after its eponymous battle, the East Sussex town is undergoing an artistic renaissance' (Forster, 2016) and in years that followed, articles by *Culture Trip* and *GQ* added Hastings to the list of towns (including nearby Margate and Folkestone) that had been deemed the 'Shoreditch' or 'Dalston-On-Sea' – two parts of London that are widely acknowledged as areas of significant gentrification (Baker, 2017; Cole, 2018).

While much work has been done to explore gentrification in urban centres, geographer Preena Shah's study on nearby St.Leonards explores and defines the particularities of gentrification in coastal towns like Hastings (2011). These changes can be understood as 'coastification', a word Shah created to describe the socio-cultural and economic transformations of the coast and the effects of in-migrants seeking the 'coastal idyll'. For Shah, the coastal idyll can be understood through a mixture of physical, economic, cultural, and social factors, including historical associations with health, wellbeing, and nature which has long been a draw to coastal towns; landscape; (comparative) housing market affordability; the mixture of heritage and regeneration; independent retail; festivals and events; alternative models of living; and the presence of creative communities.

At the Stables, Neil - who grew up in and around Hastings - stressed that Hastings has always been a creative place with creative residents, well before the Hastings Contemporary arrived. And as an aside, it has 'always been changing!'[2] Back in 1990, writer and filmmaker Jonathan Meades, while *In Search of Bohemia,* described how Hastings had been invaded by artists and questioned whether they would leave their mark on the town or whether it would leave its mark on them. Nevertheless, flagship cultural projects are often used as an attempt to construct towns as cultural or artistic places. Martin Zebracki's research on artist Banksy's temporary art project/ apocalyptic theme park *Dismaland* in Weston-Super-Mare, North Somerset (2017) and Jonathan Ward's critical study of arts led regeneration in Margate, Kent (2018) have explored this and the varying successes. Margate's rise from ageing seaside town in disrepair to 'one of the UK's most burgeoning creative scenes' is perhaps more well-known than Hastings (England's Creative Coast, 2022). Ward's study highlights how the establishment of the Turner Contemporary, an art gallery on Margate's harbour front, helped to create an 'artful brand' for Margate, while questioning its sustainability.

This idea of the 'artful brand' is interesting when reflecting on how both Hastings and Margate are two of the towns included in England's Creative Coast: a 'cultural tourism experience' that connects seven key arts organisations along the Kent, Essex, and East Sussex coast including the Turner Contemporary, Margate; Cement Fields, Gravesend; De La Warr Pavilion, Bexhill-on Sea; Metal,

Southend-on-Sea; Towner Eastbourne; Creative Folkestone and Hastings Contemporary. England's Creative Coast provides an itinerary website which allows visitors to curate their own journeys across the '1400 km of shoreline from the South Downs to the Thames Estuary' and on route, experience commissioned site-specific public artworks, accompanied by the 'world's first art Geotour' – connecting art to the landscape and local stories and memories. Being included in the project groups Hastings within a collective list of towns described by Turner Contemporary as 'thriving with creativity ... and some of the most thought-provoking contemporary art being produced today' (2022).

While visual art and design are key to these towns being understood as 'thriving with creativity', theatre is often left out of the conversation. On England's Creative Coast's website, underneath the tag 'Theatre and Cinema', only a handful of theatres are included in the list – Theatre Royal Margate, Chichester Festival Theatre, and Woodville Theatre in Gravesend. Visual art has long been associated with the coast and artists continue to play a role in the aesthetics of seaside towns: whether this is through their association with historic or existing artistic colonies or schools (for instance St. Ives and Newlyn in Cornwall) or the establishment of art galleries. Meanwhile the relationship between theatre and English coastal towns might be seen as more associated with their past, as theatre and public entertainment became an important part of the seaside resort offer.

Theatre in Hastings

In the early nineteenth century, Hastings became a resort town for the wealthy middle-classes as new railway networks across England made it easier for people to travel to and from the coast (Urquhart and Acott, 2013). It was during the 1800s that theatres started appearing throughout the town. The earliest was The Theatre which opened in 1825 and played a range of comedies, tragedies, interludes, farces, and operas until it closed in 1833 and was sold to a committee of Wesleyan Methodists and turned into a chapel. Following this came The Gaiety Theatre (1882); The Empire Theatre of Varieties (1899; later the Hippodrome Theatre and then the De Luxe Cinema) and the White Rock Pavillion (1927) built for the Hastings Municipal Orchestra. The Gaiety closed in 1932 and was converted into a cinema and is now an Odeon, and what was once the Empire Theatre of Varieties was gutted in 1978 and is currently used as a bingo hall, amusement arcade, and snooker club – named the De Luxe Leisure Centre.[3] Today the White Rock Theatre is owned by the Hastings Borough Council. With a seating capacity of 1066, it now hosts touring shows, comedy, music tribute acts, piano competitions, and musicals.

Today, theatre and performance play an important role in the impressive annual cultural programme that Hastings offers: including festivals, carnivals, and events dedicated to theatre, comedy, art, literature, storytelling, Pride, heritage, music, food and drink, pirates and folk traditions including the annual 'Jack in the Green' May Day celebration. Locally rooted projects such as *Bloom Britannia*, a 'people's opera' by Barefoot Opera, staged in 2021, brought together professional actors, musicians and singers with a chorus of people from Hastings, St. Leonards and Bexhill to explore what it means to live in a south coast, seaside town today through workshops and performance. However, as Leigh Shine a local theatre-maker who reached out to me stressed, though Hastings has attracted writers, performers, directors, and producers – there is little infrastructure for theatre-making within the town. In 2019, this led Leigh along with collaborator and local writer Lisa Harmer-Pope, and a local cast to stage their interactive play (audience members took on the role of house buyers attending an auction) *Price on Application* in a house in St. Leonards.[4]

The most recent *Culture-Led Regeneration Strategy for Hastings 2016–2021* acknowledges that while the visual arts, music, and cinema are all strong elements of the town's cultural identity, theatre is less 'well established', partly due to the limited amount of performance venues (Hastings Borough Council, 2015). In addition to the Stade – an outdoor performance space next to Hastings Contemporary – the strategy lists two theatres: the White Rock Theatre and St Mary in the Castle, a charitable trust and live music, arts, and culture venue. The Stables Theatre, while producing a dedicated theatre offer all year around, sits outside of the culture-led strategies, creative branding, and narratives of change that surround the town. But entangles with them in interesting ways. The last part of this chapter explores how the Stables has become an important resource for local theatre-makers who have started to build relationships with the completely volunteer-led theatre; utilising it as a space to perform, rehearse, and workshop. But before this, I follow the multiple lines of volunteering that weave throughout the town.

Exploring volunteering as care and creativity

Volunteers are intrinsically woven into the everyday cultural and creative fabric of Hastings. In 1989, Hastings Voluntary Action was set up to promote and support the many groups involved in voluntary action, and continues to provide training and connect people with a wide range of volunteering opportunities today. Volunteering can be an important and enjoyable, social and creative part of life for people who take part. According to *The Community Life Survey 2020/21*, approximately 28 million people in England participated in some form of voluntary activity during the 12-month period (DCMS, 2021). But volunteering is also complex. As geographer Oli Mould warns, increasingly, many vital public services (for example local libraries) are being supported and propped up by voluntary efforts as a result of austerity; where unpaid labour is 'rebranded as 'community creativity', plugging the gaps left by a necessary programme of 'living within our means'' (Mould, 2018, p. 52). This section of the chapter follows the multiple and complex lines of care and creativity that make up the meshwork of volunteering in Hastings, and opens up questions around how and where a volunteer-run theatre entangles with them.

While recent developments and strategies are helping to fuel a culture-led regeneration in Hastings, much of the town's cultural and creative life continues to be the result of voluntary effort (Hastings Borough Council, 2015). Alongside having a completely volunteer-run theatre, many independent festivals and events that make up Hastings' annual cultural programme were established and continue to be organised by volunteers, including the annual Hastings Bonfire. The members run Hastings Art Forum Gallery and the independent Electric Palace cinema are just some of the cultural spaces sustained by volunteers. Meanwhile, *Hastings Independent Press* (*HIP*), a free fortnightly newspaper is completely run by a group of local residents who voluntarily write, edit, photograph, assist with admin, and organise events. Their aim is to provide an impartial platform for political debate, regional news, and the local creative arts scene. Performances at the Stables are often (only) reviewed in *HIP* by local audience members.

These examples demonstrate volunteering as creative – contributing to the town's cultural and creative life. But interestingly, also subscribing to Hastings' reputation of being a town with a 'just do it' attitude and unconventional, independent and bohemian spirit; something that lead Jonathan Meades to visit in 1990 on a quest to find Bohemia in a post-bohemian age (In Search of Bohemia, 1990). I found these characteristics repeated throughout my research – in press, cultural strategy reports, and conversations: 'if you want to get something done in Hastings you have to do it yourself', explained Neil during our first meeting.[5] Shah refers to something similar in 'site of difference' – a phrase used to describe the feeling of alternative models of living found in coastal towns. For Shah, 'site of difference' encapsulates the 'non-conformity from more rigid societal expectations' that is often associated with coastal towns (Shah, 2011, p. 59). And is one of the ingredients that helps to create the 'coastal idyll', mentioned earlier in the chapter. Shah writes how factors including site of difference are often sold as cultural commodities which, in turn, can contribute to instances of 'coastification'.

Life in coastal towns can often exist in stark contrast to the 'coastal idyll' that surrounds them, with not everyone benefiting from the economic growth and opportunities that regeneration brings. Recently, an independent report by Chief Medical Officer for England, Chris Whitty urgently called for cross-governmental action to address the economic challenges and social levels of deprivation that coastal towns face (Whitty, 2021). A compound of slow decline of industries (domestic tourism, fishing), lack of investment, physical location, and a '180-degree hinterland' has resulted in common and shared challenges: health inequalities, precarious low-paid seasonal employment and lack of access to centres of employment, neglected public services and infrastructure, declining architecture, the effects of the climate crisis (coastal erosion and rising sea levels), and poor public transport links (Locality, 2021). In many coastal towns across England, the housing crisis continues to be a pressing issue. In Hastings, local newspapers report on the sharp increase in house prices and rents (third fastest in the country), increased buyer demand due to people seeking the 'coastal idyll', dormant second homes, and the rise of Airbnb hosts running multiple property portfolios – removing houses from the long-term rental market. This has led to forums such as 'Changing Hastings' – set up by local volunteers as a space to discuss the emotional effects of precarious living conditions and the rapid changes experienced, whilst thinking through and inviting ideas for tangible solutions.

Recent reports have highlighted how volunteers and the wider Voluntary Community and Social Enterprise (VCSE) sector are playing an important role in responding to and mitigating the effects of these challenges, while contributing to the future of coastal towns. *Power of community on the coast* (2021) by Locality – a national membership network for community organisations – reports how the VSCE sector is forging models of 'community-led coastal regeneration', whereby locally led groups are solving local issues through bottom-up initiatives. Five case study towns – Birkenhead, Merseyside; Newquay, Cornwall; Amble, Northumberland; Great Yarmouth, Norfolk and Hastings – illustrate how groups along the coast are protecting and providing local jobs and driving sustainable tourism through community-owned businesses; playing a role in supporting health and wellbeing; setting up green initiatives and supporting environmental education; and creating affordable homes and places to work through community-led ownership and development. Here, community-led regeneration can be understood as a response to the pressures of 'coastficiation' by making sure that residents benefit from regeneration strategies that focus on the visitor economy.

Much of this work can be found within Hastings' community ownership landscape, highlighted in The National Lottery Community Fund's summary report, *Hastings: From gentrification to cooperation* (Iqbal, 2021). The report draws attention to the locally rooted, 'grassroots organisations [who] are reclaiming disused and underused spaces to provide affordable opportunities for the community to live, work and thrive' (Iqbal, 2021). Heart of Hastings Community Land Trust (CLT) is one example of this. Owned by its members and supported by volunteers, it uses social investment and donations to develop land and buildings on behalf of its communities – creating genuinely affordable homes and community facilities with long-term rents tied to local incomes and capped at rates of inflation. As a CLT, and part of a wider commons (Hastings Commons Ventures), they also act as stewards, protecting community assets in perpetuity. Julian Dobson, in his 'radical agenda for the future of high-streets', sees this approach as a promising model for the future of towns, writing that by:

> … identifying buildings and places that have value and meaning within local communities and refitting them for contemporary needs, we can preserve the essential character of our town centres without fossilising them in uses and activities that are no longer appropriate
>
> (Dobson, 2015, p. 200).

The idea that townspeople can transform old buildings into community assets speaks to how the Stables Theatre was established in the early 1950s. An alliance between the newly established Old Hastings Preservation Society and the Hastings and District Theatre Guild

Figure 4.2 Stables Theatre, Hastings. Photographer: Peter Mould

– made up of multiple local amateur theatre groups – saved the 1746 stables block from being demolished and converted it into a theatre and art gallery. The Stables' archivist Sue Dengate described to me how fundraising helped to raise money for renovations and donations from local businesses and townspeople, and rope from the local fishermen, helped to decorate and equip the theatre. Janet Tachauer, a long-standing member of the Stables, remembered how 'the local community felt strongly that it was their theatre' and how many members from the immediate locality 'were supporters, rather than participants'.[6]

Volunteering is so entwined with the fabric of the Stables and with that, the feeling that – this is our theatre – still remains today in the collective pride that everything is done by volunteers. 'I think the do-it-yourself attitude of the town is reflected in the theatre' Neil explained and further added 'there is a freedom but also responsibility in that'.[7] This responsibility lies in the way that the Stables volunteers act as custodians of their building – with their membership, along with ticket sales, contributing to its upkeep – but also in the ways they steward the theatre company itself. Through their voluntary efforts, sets are constructed, pre-show glasses are filled, and lines are rehearsed, all the while keeping the 126-seat auditorium maintained and the theatre programme running. This is important when considering how cultural strategies place heavy emphasis on the daytime economy. As Julie Keeler, a box office volunteer stressed, the Stables provides 'affordable entertainment' for residents of Hastings, in the evening and all year around. 'I have looked at some stuff coming up at the White Rock Theatre on the front, and it's about £30 a person! Here, it's £13.50 and cheaper if you're a member'.[8] But what role does the theatre play for residents of the town who volunteer there?

Conversations with Stables volunteers

In October 2021, I followed the lines of care and creativity back to the theatre itself, and in this section, I reflect on conversations with volunteers who continue to offer their time, skills, knowledges, ideas, and creativity.[9] In the theatre's bar, I sat with a group of front of house, box office, kiosk and bar volunteers and heard how early retirement or voluntary redundancies had left many with time to try something new, even if they didn't feel very 'theatrical'. Others including Annie Edwards had been involved with the Stables for 40 years in various production roles before joining the front of house team. The theatre was described as a local and walkable place of social contact – somewhere to chat with friends and meet new people, especially by those who had moved to Hastings without knowing anyone or who live alone. 'If you're on your own there is always something to be done here', explained Jackie Woollaston, describing it as a place where minds can be kept active. A big draw for many was the intergenerational aspect of the place. Even though a majority of the front of house volunteers are retired, interactions with audiences and the rest of the theatre allow for conversations with people of different ages. It was also described as 'an escape' and 'a lifeline' – stories across the group of ageing and ill parents and partners, death and divorce – meant that the Stables acted as a space of respite in times of stress, heartbreak, and isolation. For many, this led to feeling part of something bigger and what was described many times as a 'feeling of community'.

Later, in conversations with a group of Stables actors, designers, technicians, writers, and directors, I learnt how volunteering had been a way of re-engaging with theatre-making after retiring or leaving professional roles in the industry. Dee Harvey, who designs sets for the Stables, used to work as a theatre designer before moving into education. Dee moved to Hastings eight years ago and joined the

Stables after receiving an email from Hastings Art Forum – a member's organisation and gallery space which aims to support and connect local artists in Hastings. It was a circulated call out for a designer to work on a Stables production and, after responding, Dee has been involved in all areas of production design for the Stables ever since. Meanwhile, Jane Richardson – who directs and stage manages – used to work as a deputy stage manager (DSM) for operas, before leaving to home to educate her children. For Jane, it was a visit to the Stables to watch her daughter perform in a local dance school's show that acted as a catalyst for her involvement in theatre again:

> I dropped her backstage… so this would have been 20 odd years after I'd done any theatre work. And it was a smell. It was smelling backstage, and it just hit that part of my brain, and I thought, I need to be here! It was extraordinary, like a physical thing. So, I rang up and said, this is me, this is what I've got, I can do these things, any good? And they said 'yes, please'. I came and stage managed a few shows and then I was able to go back into directing. I'd always wanted to go back into it for a long time. If I was still working professionally as a DSM I would never be able to be directing. You just can't make that crossover in that way. Not without a long period of time and an awful lot of work.

This feeling of the Stables being a space to try stuff out was echoed by David Manners, a writer from nearby Eastbourne. Like Dee and Jane, David had experience of working in professional theatre when he was younger – training at the Birmingham Rep and then becoming a theatre designer, working with choreographer Matthew Bourne – before pursuing a career in writing. David explained how getting involved with the Stables gave him the courage to write a script for the first time: 'I would never have braved actually putting anything on the stage. It had never occurred to me that I could even brave such a thing'. David was a winner of the Stables Theatre New Writing Competition, which gives anyone the opportunity to submit a play and, if successful, have it read or developed and staged at and by the Stables. Neil described how the ambition of the competition is to encourage and support new writing, new voices and with that new audiences – with the Stables becoming a place where new work is created in the town.

For some, the Stables has been a place to re-engage with theatre-making. For others it has been a starting point in their career. Elliott Davis first visited the Stables when working as a technician on a production of *Happenings* – a play about the lives of three 30-somethings in a seaside town - by local playwright John Berry, which visited the Stables while on tour. Elliott reached out to Neil to see if he could get involved with the theatre and ended up helping to organise the Fringe Festival at the Stables a month later. Elliott explained how as a young person, who hasn't yet been able to gain a lot of experience, the Stables has afforded the chance try out different roles:

> Being able to try everything out and do other things ... if I went straight into doing it professionally. I would be doing just one thing probably. But here, from stage managing for a production to rigging lights the week after. Two very different things. And two things that I don't think anywhere else I would get to do in such close proximity to each other.

Through these conversations, the Stables can be understood as bringing together some of the complexities of volunteering within the town – where lines of creativity and cultures of care entangle. For its volunteers, the Stables acts as a local space of care, generosity, sociability, and feeling useful in retirement. But also functions as space where

Figure 4.3 Stables Theatre backstage crew. Photographer: Cara Gray

people can come to collaborate creatively. Providing opportunities to take part, experiment, learn and expand skills and take creative risks outside of narrow disciplines.

Changing rhythms of the Stables Theatre

Before my first visit to the Stables in August 2021, I had read that the theatre was – like Hastings – going through period of 'change'. This change, or new sense of direction, was to encourage greater participation and as Neil explained - 'invite more people in'. Neil became Chair of the Stables just before the Covid19 lockdowns when, like all other theatres across the country, it had to close its doors to audiences. But this time of pause acted as an opportunity to reflect on the theatre's past whilst looking to the future in order to adapt to survive:

> During lockdowns one of my big things was to think about how we open up more to the community and actually just to get more people in here to use it, because, as I said, it was very much seen as a 'club theatre'. Historically, you had to be a member to be able to buy tickets, you had to be a member for more than 24 hours to be able to buy drinks at the bar. Anything to stop you buying a ticket and walking in, we had.[10]

The lasting reputations of the Stables came up frequently throughout my research. During the twentieth century, many amateur theatre companies began as club or membership theatres. This meant that anyone wanting to take part in or watch a performance had to be a paying member of the theatre. Today this idea might seem cliquey, but many club theatres actually had more radical roots – allowing the production of unlicensed, experimental and controversial plays that hadn't been approved by the censor at the time (Milling et al, 2018). The Stables no longer functions as a club theatre; however, the reputation still lingers, with some front of house volunteers admitting that they felt this way about the theatre before they joined. Jonathan Reed who moved to Hastings in 1987, recalled passing by the theatre for many years and thinking that it was something 'exclusive'. Meanwhile, June Hills who grew up in and around Hastings, remembered the theatre first opening in 1959, explaining how it had an 'elitist feel' in the early days:

> Hastings is a small town now but it was even smaller then. It was in the local newspapers. About the group that had got together to reinvent this place. But it kind of had this elitist feel. That if you

weren't one of these theatre groups then you didn't actually fit in. It was intimidating to walk into the place.

The Stables' history hasn't just had an effect on its reputation within the town. As Neil explained, some old ways of working within the building still lingered too. The theatre's closure afforded time and an opportunity to rethink these ways of working and with that, the theatre's role within the town: when it was used, how it was used and who it was used by. The empty building allowed for experimenting with new ways of working and 'giving it a go', as local theatre-makers and musicians reached out to use the dormant space:

> It used to open at half past ten, when the box office opened, and closed at one. You were allowed a key if you were a director. And if you were directing or rehearsing a play then you would possibly come in at seven, open the theatre until half-nine, and that was it. That was the only time the theatre was used. It just sat empty ... When we had the lockdowns, and obviously straight away everything had to shut, it gave me a baseline. And so, the first person who came to me said they were doing some R&D and would they be able to rehearse at the Stables. And I said, right, okay. The rules at the moment are that you can do R&D if you are a professional company, and so yeah come in! That's how we started breaking down and as soon as somebody heard that *they* were using the Stables, then somebody else came along and said, 'can we use the Stables?' It's sort of been like lighting the blue touch paper and just seeing what happens.

During this period, the Stables hosted a number of local professional theatre companies including Fetch Theatre, Theatre Nation, BallyBest Theatre Company, and Oyster Creatives who used the building to rehearse, experiment, and live stream performances and discussions. A group of technicians from the West End used the building for R&D and local musicians rehearsed and filmed on stage. Earlier in this chapter I reflected on the seasonal and daily rhythms of seaside towns. If we understand everyday spaces as having rhythms, as Tim Edensor highlights – some inscribed, often collective, multitude of 'habits, schedules, and routines' that become 'part of how 'we' get things done' – these new ways of working can be understood as disrupting or, as Neil described, 'breaking down' the habitual rhythm of the theatre itself (Edensor, 2016, p. 8).

Since the lockdowns, the Stables has continued to break down these habitual rhythms: looking at ways to bring people in and support the building and the theatre that is produced there. In July 2021, the sixth annual Hastings Fringe Festival – which usually takes place over a month and in multiple venues across the town – had to scale back to one venue and chose the Stables to host a wide array of new playwrights and performers. Later in August, and for the first time, the Stables became a venue for Hastings Pride Month – hosting a series of performances by LGBTQIA+ artists, and in October the building held the second annual Hastings Theatre Festival, taking place over eight days. These instances have not only brought new performers and writers in to the space, but also new audiences who have been attracted by new offers/repertoire (recently 30–50% of audiences have been non-members). Meanwhile, local theatre-makers and companies, who had been invited over the threshold, have continued to use the space alongside Stables members. As Jane described 'now you can't move for professionals, they're everywhere'.

The Stables has become an important resource for theatre-making in Hastings. This is something that I learnt after speaking to Dominique Gerrard, Patrick Kealey, and Michael Punter – three local professional theatre-makers who continue to build a relationship with the Stables.[11] I was interested to learn how they first became involved with the volunteer-led theatre – Michael, a local playwright who moved to Hastings from London 20 years ago, heard about the Stables after his agent asked whether he wanted to sell the amateur rights to his play *Darker Shores* for a Stables production; meanwhile Dominique, a director and acting coach, and Patrick, performer and creative director of Theatre Nation (one of the local theatre companies that used the Stables during lockdown), both auditioned for and performed in a Stables production of Conor McPherson's *The Weir* in 2019. 'I've lived in Hastings more than 15 years now and I never really had anything to do with the Stables because it was very much its own thing' explained Patrick:

> It was a kind of amateur theatre club, in a sense. And if you work professionally, it's kind of difficult to combine. There's sort of tensions between those two worlds, which are difficult in some ways to overcome. It's not that I didn't feel welcome, I just didn't feel like there was a way that I could contribute very much. And so that changed partly because the theatre was doing a production of *The Weir*.

Conversations led to how they were navigating their place and work within a completely volunteer-led and amateur theatre as professional theatre-makers – 'combining worlds', as Patrick described, as well as understanding the role the building plays in their work. 'In the most negative way of putting it across, we are fighting to the death over the use of this space' explained Dominique about local theatre-makers' emerging relationships with the Stables:

> Of course, that's a sort of glib joke really. But it's why it's so in demand. And we've all had many conversations about finding and cultivating and helping to transform any other spaces. And yes, Hastings has a big live music scene but finding a space that could be a dedicated theatre space ... there is a lack there.

As mentioned earlier on in this chapter, there is a feeling that Hastings lacks the theatre infrastructure for the number of theatre-makers that live and work there. And this feeling was one that was reiterated in our conversation. Patrick followed by describing how having an ongoing relationship with a dedicated space in the town can also provide a sense of stability and credibility to small local theatre companies like as his own:

> I don't feel anymore that I'm out on a limb. I feel that the building is somewhere I can call home. What I do is not to everybody's taste but there are enough people who respect what my theatre company is trying to do and so having a base is very, very important. I think you have to feel you have a home somewhere. You know, what they say – home is the place where if you turn up at the door, they have to let you in. And I feel that very, very much here. That was the biggest shift for me.

This stability and credibility – the feeling of having a 'base' or a 'home' that access to a building provides – is something that Patrick described as being vital to theatre-makers. Not only as a regular venue to perform in, but also in the moments surrounding the performance itself. When applying for funding: 'we can now say to a potential funding bid, we have a theatre that supports this project! And they support us in kind' Patrick explained. Meanwhile, having the Stables as a base has also provided opportunities to invite other people over the threshold. In September 2020, Theatre Nation invited theatre director David Glass (from David Glass Ensemble) to host his five-stage creative practice workshop 'Alchemy Extraordinary' at the Stables. This relationship and collaboration continued in June 2022 with a six-show run of Samuel Beckett's *Waiting for Godot* and a series of Godot text-based skills workshops.

Alongside the excitement around the evolving role of the Stables – and how it might continue to provide a space to perform as well as rehearse, experiment, and workshop for local theatre-makers – there was also an understanding and sensitivity expressed about potentially using the space too much, as Dominique discussed:

> I'm really aware that we're going great, this building's open to us now! Because, just to be really practical and mercenary for a minute, the professional art scene has got no money. So, we're all desperately scrambling around for resources and space. But there are also people who want to use this building for their hobby ... Are we stealing the space away? How do we share that? Would I love this to be a place of experimentation, where there are workshops and different things going on every week? Yes, of course. But then would it be able to serve its members? We want there to be this hybrid, we want there to be a collaboration.

Dominique's acknowledgement of taking up time and space within the building, along with her call for a sense of hybridity and collaboration, made me reflect on Ingold's idea of the meshwork. While some theatre-makers and companies might use the Stables for one-off performances, as a receiving house for a touring show or a venue for a festival, many – including Dominique, Michael, and Patrick – continue to build ongoing relationships with the Stables through the spaces they use and the time they spend there. As a result of these ongoing relationships – through the work that they make, the time that they spend and the ideas/activities that they bring – they can be understood as new and multiple 'threads' or 'forces and flows of material' pouring into the building with the potential to entangle with what is already happening there (Ingold, 2010, p. 10). 'The thing' Ingold writes, 'is not just one thread but a certain gathering together of the threads of life'. If we consider the theatre (building and company) as a 'thing' then it is never finished, but in a constant state of becoming through the entanglement or gathering of threads: 'as they move through time and encounter one another, the trajectories of diverse constituents are bundled together in diverse combinations' (Ingold, 2010, p. 11).

Towards a hybrid theatre?

> We always say it's not an amateur theatre, it's a citizen's theatre. It's genuine, it's got a little Athenian model to it
> (Interview with Michael Punter, 11 October 2021).

Over the course of my research, this call for a hybridity and collaboration at the Stables slowly started to emerge in many diverse combinations. While the Stables Theatre continues to produce its own ten productions throughout the year through complete voluntary effort, alongside outside professional and amateur companies who increasingly use the venue to stage performances through varying box office percentage splits – there have been moments of entanglement, experiment and new ways of working together. In November 2021 the Stables staged *The Incident at Marshfell*, a haunting play set on the marshes in East Sussex, written by Michael Punter, directed by Dominique Gerrard, and crowdfunded by their newly formed theatre company Vital Theatre. The cast comprised of two professional actors but I was excited to see many familiar names from the Stables in the programme – including set construction by Mike Willard (also a front of house volunteer), lighting design by Elliot Davis, and photography and videography (and a ghostly appearance) by resident photographer Peter Mould. Michael was also commissioned by the Stables to write an adaptation of Hans Christian Anderson's *The Snow Queen* for their 2021 Christmas production of the same name. 'He didn't charge us royalties but we did pay him to write the script', explained Neil, 'but he probably didn't get paid as much as someone having a play put on professionally'. More recently David Manners' play *Here at Last is Love* – which documents untold stories of gay lives during World War II London – was performed by a cast of Stables members (including David) and directed by Jason Morrell, in a partnered production between the Stables Theatre and BallyBest Productions (David's theatre company), sponsored by Hastings Pride.

In February 2022, Neil described how navigating these new ways of working continues to be a lesson in 'just giving it a go'.[12] The emerging moments of hybridity within the Stables has not only meant experiments in working together but has also called for a deeper understanding of the building itself. 'Now I'm saying if you're thinking of using the Stables regularly – put some roots down and learn a little bit more about how the theatre works'. So far, this has meant encouraging theatre companies to bring their own technicians and commit to learning from the Stables technicians about how the particular equipment and space works. All productions usually get the assistance of the

Stables technical team and so 'if they learn how to use the building, it becomes so much easier to schedule them into the season because there will always be someone who knows how to run the lighting' Neil explained.[13] On the day that I met Neil, a production of *Hitleria Pizzeria*, an absurdist drama set in Serbia and written by local writer, producer and performer John Knowles, was being performed at the Stables that night – and live streamed – as part of 2022 Serbian Month. Neil explained how the stage manager for *Hitleria Pizzeria* had volunteered to be the assistant stage manager for the Stables production of Shakespeare's *Macbeth*, that had run for eight dates the previous month. 'She did it purely to get to know the stage' Neil explained 'and it's also meant that she has now become a member'.

It is important, however, to highlight how slippery, and sometimes unhelpful, these distinctions between 'professional' and 'amateur' are. As Peter Mould exclaimed during my conversations with volunteers – 'aren't we all theatre-makers?!' Many people who audition and perform in the Stables Theatre's own productions have or continue to act as paid professionals at other times, or have trained professionally at some point of their life. As Neil reflected on the cast of *Here at Last is Love:* 'the cast are all members of the theatre although one also has an international career. But the rest of us don't, in fact, three of us are running box office this morning.'[14] Meanwhile, as explored earlier in this chapter, many of the Stables Theatre's production team either have professional theatre backgrounds and training, or are starting out in their theatre careers and using the Stables as a platform. Alongside this, people bring their various skills, knowledges, and ideas from professions that are not specifically connected to theatre but can be applied to theatre-making in various ways. Mike Willard, who runs the bar and is part of the set building team, brings skills from a career in engineering – reflected in the general repairs that he assists with throughout the building, and in the magic he creates on stage. The table that Mike designed and built for *The Incident at Marshfell* floated on stage with no strings or wires in site.

While many amateur theatre-makers strongly identify as 'amateur' – rejecting its derogative associations and embracing the freedom to participate in multiple roles and the creativity of making theatre with limited materials and space (Gray, 2020) – design scholar Stephen Knott's work on the amateur craftsperson provides a useful lens here (Knott, 2015). Knott writes how 'amateur' does not describe a person, or skill level, but a spatial-temporal state 'where one loves the activity that is being undertaken, and would do it anyway, voluntarily, under no duress' (Knott, 2013). 'It is about different financial expectations' Neil noted, when reflecting on the multiple layers of theatre-making that are emerging at the Stables.

These multiple layers can be understood as blurring the lines that disconnect the 'professional' and 'amateur'. Nicholson writes that this 'formal disconnect', found in the theatre sector, often means 'amateurs have limited opportunities to extend their knowledge of theatre craft by learning from and alongside professionals'; while calling for new models of participation where amateur, professional, and community theatre-makers can work with and learn from each other (Nicholson, 2020, p. 306). The Royal Shakespeare Company's Open Stages initiative can be understood as an experiment in this. A project that saw professional theatre-makers work with around 300 amateur theatre companies – through workshops, masterclasses, and mentoring – to stage Shakespeare, or Shakespeare-inspired work. Molly Flynn observed that by sharing space, resources, and approaches, there were two-way transmissions of learning. Amateur theatre-makers developed skills commonly taught in professional spaces whilst also feeling an increased sense of affirmation that their labour and dedication had a cultural value (Flynn, 2017). Meanwhile professional practitioners gained an insight into the vitality of self-sustaining performance outside the structures of the industry, 'made by those who do not depend on the practice for their day-to-day income' (Flynn, 2017, p. 496). Flynn's observations spoke to the ambition of a hybrid theatre as described by Dominique Gerrard – as a potential space that facilitates exchange, but in this case – one which is volunteer-led:

> We're all here to learn from each other. Because as we know, learning doesn't just go one way. Learning is a thing that happens in the room, it's not a one-way process. But how does one go about cultivating that? Maybe the trick about a hybrid theatre is making it somewhere that has a space for everybody ... I believe that an organisation needs an ethos and if I were running this building my ethos would be – we need to all learn together.

In this chapter I have sought to explore the role of volunteer-led theatres by understanding how they entangle and are sustained by the meshworks of their towns. Using the idea of meshwork as a tool helps imagine a theatre entangling with multiple lines (people, ideas, skills, challenges, cultural strategies, happenings) that reach both *from* and *out* into the town – sometimes circling back, sometimes colliding or weaving with others. Some missing the theatre completely but intertwining with ones that do.

The seasonal and daily rhythms of coastal towns mean that the focus often lies on the daytime visitor economy, but volunteer-led theatres contribute to the cultural and creative life of residents who live in seaside towns throughout the year. They can provide spaces to socialise and feel useful; of care and artistic experimentation; a place where people have re-engaged with theatre-making after retiring from it professionally, or where careers in theatre are getting started. But they can also be places of possibility. By inviting local companies, performers, and playwrights into the building – alongside their own work – the Stables is creating a space in Hastings that supports new and multiple forms of theatre-making and repertoire; what Michael Punter likened to a 'shocking library' where audiences might not know what they're going to experience. And where new ways of working are complicating formal distinctions between amateur and professional theatre(s).

A hybrid theatre model is emerging where amateur/volunteer and professional makers not only share space but sometimes experiment with making theatre together. This chapter has offered a glimpse into those moments of mutual learning and exchange which opens up bigger questions around the possibilities and futures of volunteer-led theatres. Specifically, how the scale of a town has the potential to support such entanglements, hybridity, and spaces. Spaces that are reliant on making and sustaining connections and long-term relationships. At the time of writing, the Stables continues to make connections throughout the town – collaborating with other theatre companies, new writers, the local Bexhill College (through informal apprenticeships), and the Refugee Buddy Project, a local refugee and migrant-led organisation, who recently held a fundraising evening of music and spoken word at the Stables. Meanwhile, other activities including baby groups, art classes, acting workshops, and sound baths have also been invited into the space. This chapter captures a small moment in the life of the Stables Theatre and of Hastings, and, as I write this – they are evolving still.

Notes

1 Interview with Neil Sellman, Hastings, 23 August 2021.
2 Interview with Neil Sellman, Hastings, 15 February 2022.
3 History of theatres in Hastings from arthurlloyd.co.uk (Accessed, 20 September 2021).
4 Interview with Leigh Shine, 22 October 2021.
5 Interview with Neil Sellman, Hastings, 23 August 2021.

6 Email from Janet Tachauer, 11 October 2021.
7 Interview with Neil Sellman, Hastings 23 August 2021.
8 Members of the Stables Theatre and under 18s pay a discounted rate of £8.50 for Stables Theatre productions. From conversations with volunteers, Hastings 11 October 2021.
9 Conversations with Stables volunteers, Hastings, 11 and 12 October 2021. All related quotations.
10 Interview with Neil Sellman, Hastings, 23 August 2021. All related quotations.
11 Interviews with local professional theatre-makers, Hastings, 11 October 2021. All related quotations.
12 Interview with Neil Sellman, Hastings 15 February 2022.
13 Currently, there are conversations about the potential future payment of Stables in-house technicians by outside companies – if they need their expertise on a production – further complicating the distinctions between theatre-making.
14 Email from Neil Sellman, 20 June 2022.

References

Baker, C. (2017). 'Why Hastings Is the Shoreditch Of Sussex and the UK's New Art Hotspot', *Culture Trip*, 1 November [Online]. Available at: theculturetrip.com/europe/united-kingdom/england/articles/why-hastings-is-the-shoreditch-of-sussex-and-the-uk-s-new-art-hotspot/ (Accessed 19 October 2021).

Bussell, H and Forbes, D. (2006). "Friends' Schemes in Arts Marketing: Developing Relationships in British Provincial Theatres', *International Journal of Arts Management*, 8(2), pp. 38–49.

Campbell, S. (2015). 'An Insider's Guide to Hastings', *Condé Nast Traveller*, 4 February [Online]. Available at: cntraveller.com/gallery/insider-guide-hastings (Accessed 19 October 2021).

Cole, O. (2018). 'How Hastings became 'Dalston-On-Sea'', *GQ*, 13 May [Online]. Available at: gq-magazine.co.uk/article/travel-hastings-guide (Accessed 19 October 2021).

Day, E. (2008). 'Art's a burning issue here', *The Observer*, 9 November [Online]. Available at: theguardian.com/artanddesign/2008/nov/09/hastings-art-gallery (Accessed 19 October 2021).

DCMS. (2021). *Community Life Survey 2020/21*. Available at: https://www.gov.uk/government/statistics/community-life-survey-202021 (Accessed 16 January 2022).

Dobson, J. (2015). *How to Save Our Town Centres: A Radical Agenda for the Future of High Streets*. University of Bristol: Policy Press.

Dyckhoff, T. (2012). 'Let's move to Old Town, Hastings, East Sussex', *The Guardian*, 18 May [Online]. Available at: theguardian.com/money/2012/may/18/lets-move-hastings-east-sussex (Accessed 19 October 2021).

Edensor, T. (2016). 'Introduction: Thinking About Rhythm and Place' in Edensor, T. (eds.), *Geographies of Rhythm Nature, Place, Mobilities and Bodies*. Oxon: Routledge.

Edensor, T. and Millington, S. (2013). 'Blackpool Illuminations: Revaluing Local Cultural Production, Situated Creativity and Working-Class Values', *International Journal of Cultural Policy*, 19(2), pp. 145–161.

England's Creative Coast. (2022). Culture lover's fix – Margate. Available at: https://www.englandscreativecoast.com/itineraries/culture-lover-s-fix-margate/ (Accessed 16 January 2022).

Flynn, M. (2017). 'Amateur Hour: Culture, Capital, and the Royal Shakespeare Company's Open Stages initiative', *Research in Drama Education: The Journal of Applied Theatre and Performance*, 22(4), pp. 482–499.

Forster, K. (2016). 'Creativity in Hastings: Designers Do Like to Be Beside the Seaside', *The Guardian*, 13 August [Online]. Available at: theguardian.com/lifeandstyle/2016/aug/13/creativity-in-hastings-designers-do-like-be-beside-the-seaside (Accessed 19 October 2021).

Gray, C. (2020). 'The Repairer and the Ad Hocist: Understanding the 'ongoingness' of the Amateur Theatre maker's craft', *Performance Research*, 25(1), pp. 88–95.

Hastings Borough Council (2015) *Culture-Led Regeneration Strategy for Hastings 2016–2021*. Available at: hastings.gov.uk/content/my_council/consultations/current_consultations/pdfs/Hastings_Culture-Led_Regeneration_Strategy_2016-21.pdf (Accessed: 16 October 2021).

House of Lords Select Committee (2019) *Select Committee on Regenerating Seaside Towns and Communities: The future of seaside towns*. Available at: publications.parliament.uk/pa/ld201719/ldselect/ldseaside/320/32002.htm (Accessed 15 October 2021).

In Search of Bohemia (1990), BBC TV.

Ingold, T. (2010). 'Bringing Things to Life: Creative Entanglements in a World of Materials', *Realities Working Paper 15*, Manchester: ESRC National Centre for Research Methods.

Ingold, T. (2016). *Lines: a Brief History*. London: Routledge.

Iqbal, T. (2021). *Hastings: From Gentrification to Cooperation*. [Online]. Available at: tnlcommunityfund.org.uk/insights/differences-we-make/difference-we-make/place-based-stories/hastings-from-gentrification-to-cooperation (Accessed 1 November 2021).

Knott, S. (2013). 'Reconsidering Amateur Photography: The Amateur State', Either/And. Available at: eitherand.org/reconsidering-amateur-photography/the-amateur-state/ (Accessed 21 January 2021).

Knott, S. (2015). *Amateur Craft: History and Theory*. London: Bloomsbury Academic.

Lefebvre, H. (1992(2004)). *Rhythmanalysis: Space, Time and Everyday Life*, Translated by Elden, S & Moore, G, London: continuum.

Locality (2021). *Power of Community on the Coast* [Online]. Available at: locality.org.uk/wp-content/uploads/2021/02/Power-of-community-on-the-coast-FINAL.pdf (Accessed 1 November 2021).

Milling, J., Nicholson, H. and Holdsworth, N. (2018). 'Valuing Amateur Theatre' in Nichsolson, H., Holdsworth, N. and Milling, J. (2018). *Ecologies of Amateur Theatre*. London: Palgrave Macmillan.

Mould, O. (2018). *Against Creativity*. London: Verso.
Nicholson, H. (2020). 'Labours of Social Inclusion: Amateur, Professional, Community theatres', *Studies in Theatre and Performance*, 40(3), pp. 303–308.
Nicholson, H., Holdsworth, N. and Milling, J. (2018). *Ecologies of Amateur Theatre*. London: Palgrave Macmillan.
Oppenheim, M. (2016). 'The British Creative Paradise You Haven't Heard About', *i-D*, 12 April [Online]. Available at: i-d.vice.com/en_uk/article/d3vq4x/the-british-creative-paradise-you-havent-heard-about (Accessed 20 October 2021).
Shah, P. (2011). *Coastal Gentrification: The Coastification of St Leonards-on-Sea*, PhD, Loughborough University.
Urquhart, J. and Acott, T. (2013). 'Constructing 'The Stade': Fishers' and Non-Fishers' Identity and Place Attachment in Hastings, South-East England', *Marine Policy*, 37, pp. 45–54.
Ward, J. (2018). 'Down by the Sea: Visual Arts, Artists and Coastal Regeneration,' *International Journal of Cultural Policy*, 24(1), pp. 121–138.
Whitty, C. (2021). *Chief Medical Officer's annual report 2021: health in coastal communities*, [Online] (accessed 25 July 2021).
Zebracki, M. (2018). 'Regenerating a Coastal Town Through Art: Dismaland and the (l)imitations of Antagonistic Art Practice in the City', *Cities*, 77, pp. 21–32.

5 Made to Connect
Theatrical Exchange between Town and City

Gemma Edwards

On Saturday 7 August 2021, the steam engine fired up in Spinners Mill, a grade II listed double cotton mill in the town of Leigh, Greater Manchester. This engine, restored to full working order in 2015, was last used to power the town during the 1973 Miners' Strike and is now the main attraction of the mill's Heritage Centre. I was in the engine room that Saturday watching KIT Theatre's *Digital Ghost Hunt* which had its premiere at the Den in Leigh, a fortnight of performance events put on by Manchester's leading producing theatre, the Royal Exchange, as part of their Local Exchange programme. This programme sees the Royal Exchange Theatre create partnerships with a range of community and cultural organisations over the course of a four-year residency in a town, ward, or neighbourhood in Greater Manchester. The focal point of this residency is the festival programmed by a team of specially recruited community leaders in the Royal Exchange's theatre-in-the-round peripatetic theatre space, The Den, with the aim of developing a meaningful exchange of live theatre and performance between city and region.

While most of the performances took place in the Den – which was housed under the bale store just outside of the mill – KIT Theatre's *Digital Ghost Hunt* was an immersive children's show which was made specifically for the building. Tasked with finding a ghostly presence, the children followed the signals on their hand-held 'ghost detectors' around the spaces of the mill, which picked up messages and clues left in ultraviolet paint. This eventually brought them to the engine room where the ghost of Stanley, a former millworker who was killed when operating this very machinery, waited behind the engine. Part of the children's brief became to seek justice for Stanley, whose name had been maligned by the mill managers asserting that he was drunk at work, when, in fact, they were negligent, and the machinery was faulty. This truth is something that the children gradually piece together over the course of the show, a journey

DOI: 10.4324/9781003308058-5

which is carefully facilitated by Deputy Undersecretary Quill and the Junior Agents of the Ministry of Real Paranormal Hygiene (MORPH). Although Stanley's story is fictional, it was loosely based on a real accident that occurred in the mill in 1920, highlighting the site-specificity of the production. As the children righted the historical record, literally rewriting Stanley's story on the wall of the engine room, he descended the stairs and expressed his gratitude by tipping his hat and waving to the children as the engine kicked back into life.

Digital Ghost Hunt is a production that is centred on connection and exchange. As a piece of immersive, site-specific children's theatre, the show connected past and present, heritage and performance, and, in doing so, offered future generations a creative encounter with the historical legacies of production in their town. This theme of connection is one that I develop across the course of this chapter, where I maintain a focus on The Den in Leigh, asking how the city-based Royal Exchange Theatre connected with audiences in this town. The chapter uses 'exchange' as a keyword to explore the relationship between theatres in towns and cities, but specifically, to articulate the relationship between theatre production in the city of Manchester and post-industrial towns in the Greater Manchester region. After its pilot year in Rochdale in 2017, the Den was based in Stalybridge in 2019, Leigh in 2021 (scheduled for 2020 but delayed due to COVID-19), and Cheetham Hill in 2022. Here, I turn to the Den in Leigh (2021), drawing on ethnographic and archival research to trace performance practice as a nodal point for conceptualising alternative kinds of cultural and social exchanges between town and city.

Leigh, a town in the borough of Wigan, is historically connected to the nearby cities of Salford, Manchester, and Liverpool – and surrounding villages and towns – through its textile and mining industries. In this sense, the town is explored here as a hub of economic exchange across networks of coal, cotton, and canals that take in socioeconomic communities of various scales and shapes. Leigh is a town that was built to make, and goods that travelled along those roads, railways, and canals to central markets in the city, include: fustian in the seventeenth century, a heavy corduroy cloth worn by workers which became the chosen garments of radicals in the Chartist era; silk and cotton in the eighteenth and nineteenth centuries; and up until the 1980s, coal.

After a series of economic shocks – effected by deindustrialisation and decades of austerity measures – Leigh, like many other towns in Greater Manchester and across the UK more broadly, is grappling with its post-industrial identity. Returning to the idea of exchange, Leigh has lost its connection to the city via coal, cotton, and canals in that the coal and cotton industries are gone, and it is the largest town in the North West without a connection to a rail network. The closure of the town's industries has resulted in significant job losses, and Leigh is dominated by a retail economy, with a total of eight supermarkets springing up in the town's boundaries. Calling on one of the keywords of this book, the *civic* structures that made Leigh have been forced to adapt into new shapes and forms, although the extant legacy of those structures still plays a significant role. For example, the skeleton of Leigh's industrial culture remains visible in the town's topography: from the pit headstocks at the Lancashire Mining Museum in Astley Green, the Miner's Welfares that are still open, the massive hulking mills, and the countless estates of connected terraced houses. The streets in this town and in the villages that surround it were made to be connected, but it is not clear what is connecting them anymore.

This history of change is reflected in the town's political transitions. A former Labour heartland that voted Tory for the first time in its electoral history in 2019, Leigh figures as one of the 'left behind' towns that is central to the Conservatives' 'levelling up' agenda. In wider cultural terms, Arts Council England (ACE) identified the Wigan borough as a 'Priority Place' (2021–2024), an area where '[ACE's] investment and engagement is too low, and opportunity for [them] to effectively increase investment and engagement is high' (Arts Council England website, 2022). The Wigan borough is also listed as one of ACE's parallel programme, Levelling Up for Culture Places (2022–2026), which came from the 2022 Levelling Up White Paper where the government made a commitment to 'identifying over 100 levelling up priority places outside of London that will be the focus for additional Arts Council England engagement and investment [£43.5 million]' (HM Government, 2022). What is clear is that Leigh – like many other post-industrial towns in the UK – is caught in a dynamic in which it is being addressed, funded, and figured out by cultural policy made in metropolitan centres. This distance between metropolitan-made cultural policy and the towns that it is designed for can speak in problematic ways to the particularities of those places and communities, flattening out the distinctive cultural ecologies that already exist.

As a town of makers and innovators – a historic centre of production – there are local fears that Leigh might lose its distinctiveness and become a commuter suburb of Wigan or Salford, with the Leigh-Salford-Manchester transit scheme that opened in 2013 reconnecting the town by bus to the cities that it used to supply. Leigh has a distinctive and resilient cultural ecology which reflects the rich histories of making in the town. The tactile nature of cultural production in Leigh is captured in a number of small businesses already resident in the site of the Den and *Digital Ghost Hunt*, Spinners Mill, including contemporary artist, Lancashire Forager, who makes their art with upcycled and collected objects from the town, and Cobalt Creations, who makes handmade gifts from his shed. As one local artist who is based at Spinners Mill told me, it is precisely due to the lack of interest from investors and limited public subsidy that the town has developed this hybrid creative economy. The lack of external investment means that there is space for artists to produce work in ways driven by locality, evidencing a grassroots cultural ecology that relies on local communities to buy in, provide, and sustain a creative infrastructure.

Spinners Mill is a prime example of this rich blend of local cultural activity. Across its 2900 square metres that spans four floors, it houses a number of community organisations, including the Heritage Centre, Leigh Film Factory (community cinema), and Leigh Hackspace, leading many to call the space the 'millage' where a number of like-minded Leigh locals can meet and share their craft.[1] As part of its business model, Spinners also offers affordable rent for local businesses: it advertises this on its website as 'a hub for local Leigh companies to develop and serve their community' (Leigh Spinners Mill website, 2022). The provision of affordable studio space also enables the creation of a cluster of micro businesses that reflect a range of cultural practices. For example, Spinners Mill is home to A Will and a Way, an established acting school run by actor, Will Travis; Supernatural Diaries, an escape room in the mill run by psychic medium Tony

Figure 5.1 Spinners Mill, Leigh. Photographer: Image Village

Hindley alongside a team of paranormal investigators and actors; Pool of Life, a boxing studio; and The Music Centre which offers music lessons as well as hosting music and spoken word events.

The mill is located within a wider cultural scene in Leigh which is loosely organised in similar clusters of activity. While St Joseph's Players, one of Leigh's amateur theatre companies has been playing to local audiences since 1850, the new dance company, WigLe Dance (est. 2015) who danced for Little Amal (see Chapter 1) is growing in size, offering opportunities to young people across the Wigan borough to learn a range of dance styles and work with choreographers from further afield. The town also has an art gallery, The Turnpike, which has shifted between the hands of local authorities and local volunteers in recent history and sits on its civic square, just across from the town hall which is now home to the Local Studies unit after the council moved, controversially, to Wigan as part of the reshaping of the borough.[2] This varied arts landscape – made up of organisational cultures that extend across small businesses, freelance artists, and the amateur sector – attests to the resilience of cultural life in Leigh, which, I argue, speaks to its industrial past, its ability to innovate, adapt, and make do and mend. This chapter uses Leigh's legacies of material exchange as a way of thinking about the links between past, present, and future cultural practice in the town, positioning these tactile histories as what Raymond Williams would term a 'resource of hope' for the next generation (Williams, 1988, p. 1).

Here, I explore how the performance culture in a town (Leigh) and a producing theatre in a city (Manchester) found points of exchange, contact, and connection, alongside moments of misfire and missed opportunity. Focusing on KIT theatre's *Digital Ghost Hunt* as a performance that engaged with the particularities of the place of Leigh and its industrial legacies, the chapter highlights the ways that this piece of site-specific theatre traces and mobilises these genealogies of connection through its tactile production. In doing so, I work with the concept of 'social haunting' (Gordon, 2008; Simpson, 2021), linking this performance to the historical context of the town in ways that both challenge and deepen simplistic constructions of exchange. In *Ghostly Matters*, Avery Gordon positions social haunting as a counter-hegemonic form of sociological analysis. Rather than making use of positivist methods – which capture and analyse what is present – Gordon argues that it is important to study what is missing: she writes that 'to study social life, one must confront the ghostly aspects of it' (Gordon, 2008, p. 7). In this sense, Gordon calls for a fuller way of working with historical material – a way of looking that appreciates the social world/s as constituted by presences and absences. Taking Gordon's invitation to look for 'the ghostly signals that flash from the traffic', this chapter tells a different story of material and cultural production in a post-industrial English town – including one that acknowledges the town's colonial connections and mines the past to look to the future (Gordon, 2008, p. 192).

Local exchange: City-town connections

City-based theatre companies in England have a long history of developing relationships with people and places beyond city borders, and there are a number of examples of programmes of activity, both now and historically, that illustrate these city-region exchanges. From the National Theatre's large-scale nationwide programme Public Acts (2017–) to Nottingham Playhouse's Roundabout (1973–2010), a permanent theatre in education company which formed partnerships with schools in the East Midlands, city theatres in England have long been working across a broad geographic remit, building relationships with community, cultural, and educational institutions in towns and villages across the nation. Public Acts reflects the National Theatre's historical roots, which can be traced back to the influence of the British Drama League (1919–1990) in the conceptualisation of a national theatre in England in the 1940s, and Public Works, a programme set up by one of the leaders of civic theatre in the US, Joe Papp, in New York in the 1950s (Public Works website, 2022).[3] These historical examples of theatre's civic role – and importantly, its ability to facilitate cultural exchanges of different kinds – shape Public Acts which takes inspiration from Public Works' programmes, such as Shakespeare in the Park (Public Works website, 2022), by engaging community stakeholders in large-scale productions. Arguably, the UK 2016 EU Referendum offered a moment which renewed the significance of this long-term practice of looking beyond the city, and stimulated theatre companies in cities to look again at the ways in which they engaged with people and places outside of their immediate metropolitan contexts. This notion is explored by Vicky Featherstone, who argues that the Referendum itself constituted a kind of 'rude awakening' for theatre makers based in cities. As Artistic Director of the Royal Court in London (England), she claimed that 'as a country, we are paying more attention to the stories that are being told outside of city centres' (Featherstone quoted in Trueman, 2018). This is not only a representational question of what types of stories are being told but also a question of the site and means of production: where are these stories shared and how are they made?

The launch of Local Exchange and Public Acts coincided with this political moment, with the Royal Exchange Theatre setting up Local Exchange in 2017 and the National Theatre opening Public Acts in the same year. Although these programmes had periods of development that preceded the Referendum in 2016, these two examples highlight the different ways that metropolitan theatre companies are working to establish sustainable models of partnership with community and arts organisations beyond the city. Situating themselves in a broader geographic and cultural frame, Public Acts and Local Exchange engage meaningfully with the different senses of place that make up England's regions in a way that extends beyond models of exchange based on touring. Yet, it is worth pointing out that city-town relationships tend to be asymmetric in nature. This is not just a question of size and scale: cultural organisations in cities and towns tend to have different sets of priorities and ways of working, and these may not easily map onto each other. As I explore in this chapter via Gordon's mechanism of social haunting, towns are materially shaped in the present by their own histories, but also by legacies of previous city-town partnerships. This presents a number of key challenges for any city-based organisation working in a town: these organisations need to be attentive to the cultural ecologies that already exist in place, the political complexities and historical forces that shape them, and material concerns – such as transport networks – which might mean that culture is accessed differently in towns than it is in cities. Questions of identity between city and town cultures – and related codes of relationship and behaviour – are also important here. For example, city-based artists might make assumptions about what kinds of creative practice and imaginative potential exist in towns. These kinds of assumptions risk reproducing asymmetrical relationships where city-based artists behave as cultural providers and potentially 'bad guests' in towns, rather than recognising townspeople as cultural producers in their own right. I want to take forward this idea of a metropolitan theatre organisation seeking to change the way theatre is created, produced, and shared by working beyond its place in the city in my analysis of the Royal Exchange Theatre's Local Exchange programme. How is this city-based theatre company navigating these challenges when working in towns in Greater Manchester, and how does the Den in Leigh in 2021 evidence learning from this wider city/region relationship?

Local Exchange is a series of residencies designed to develop a true exchange of theatre and cultural activity from city to town, and town to city, in the Greater Manchester region. The programme is supported by a number of principal funders, including the Greater

Manchester Combined Authority, Arts Council England, the Esmée Fairbairn Foundation, and the Oglesby Charity Trust, who gifted the Den to the Royal Exchange Theatre which now plays a central role in the delivery of Local Exchange. Describing the programme on their website, the Royal Exchange Theatre state that it aims to 'build upon existing partnerships, develop new connections and bring together people, places and artists to cement long-lasting relationships with the communities right outside our doors' (Royal Exchange Theatre website, 2022). In this sense, the model works to decentralise the building-based practices of the Royal Exchange in favour of a more dispersed geographic model where performances are programmed beyond the city's borders. This is also a socioeconomic concern, with questions of access, participation, and inclusion being central to the selection process. The towns chosen – Stalybridge, Leigh, and Rochdale thus far – each reflect areas which have historically received lower levels of cultural investment from both ACE and cultural organisations located in Manchester city centre. Over the course of each four-year residency, the Royal Exchange Theatre work alongside existing arts organisations in the area and at neighbourhood level, including with schools, charities, libraries, and small businesses, in order to share its resources and work towards the Den, the two-week programme of performance events that takes place in the second year. The programme is co-designed by the community producers at the Royal Exchange and a team of Local Exchange Ambassadors, who are members of the community that work with the theatre to design and deliver events that best suit their hometown. Ambassador recruitment takes place via an open call in the first year of consultation and the role is voluntary, with Ambassadors often spanning across ages, professions, and backgrounds, offering a range of experiences and expertise. For example, in the case of the Leigh Ambassadors, these included the director of Leigh Film Society, a first-year university student, and the leader of the community group Everything Human Rights, who work with migrants new to the borough.

Local Exchange's four-year model was developed from a pilot project in Rochdale in 2017 where the team found that a year of consultation was needed before the delivery of the programme. In this consultation year, the theatre meets with the key cultural providers for the town – in the case of Rochdale, this was the network Link for Life which cuts across arts, health, and sport – in addition to local cultural groups that already exist in place. Inga Hirst (2021) – Director of Relationships and Engagement at the Royal Exchange Theatre and one of the designers of the Local Exchange programme – explained that the ambassador model was one way of ensuring the situatedness of this work so that the theatre could, in her terms, 'work with the cultural provision which is already there'. This collaborative journey between the Ambassadors and the Royal Exchange Theatre is centred on creating and actioning a 'manifesto for change' – a document made by the Ambassadors which details how this partnership can bring about change in the place that they call home. In addition to the programme's legacy year – where the ambassadors lead and budget a follow-up project from start to finish – the idea is that Local Exchange (and the networks it facilitates) will never leave a community and will continue to return to different towns in Greater Manchester, cycling back and forth to continue to develop these city-region relationships. Reflecting on the four-year rolling programme – and the movement of work from city to town and town to village that it enables – Hirst (2021) notes that the long-term aim is that Local Exchange, as a central part of the theatre's structure, will facilitate 'learning about communities [across Greater Manchester] that might influence central programming' of the theatre building in the city centre. This exchange has started to take place: the community-made play *No Such Thing as Ordinary* which was made in collaboration with playwright Rachel Murray as part of Stalybridge's legacy year in 2020, was first performed at the Guide Bridge Theatre in Audenshaw in October 2021 and then at the Royal Exchange's Studio in March 2022. Although this play is a cultural product which moved from the region to the city centre, the movement of this work constituted a tour. The question remains, then, whether this city-town exchange really flows two ways: does work in the region impact on the actual decision-making and institutional culture of the theatre in the city centre?

The Den in Leigh

Initially planned for the summer of 2020, the residency in Leigh was affected by COVID restrictions, meaning that audience numbers at the Den in August 2021 were limited due to the social distancing measures that were in place. Yet despite these challenges, the Den presented a rich offer of theatre and performance over the course of its two-week stay. The programme, carefully curated by the Ambassadors, in collaboration with Philippa Crossman (Community Producer at the Royal Exchange Theatre) and Carys Williams (Engagement Lead at the Royal Exchange Theatre), boasted a range of genres for all ages. This included: spoken word by Afshan D'souza-Lodhi, Channique Sterling-Brown, Amina Beg, and Tom Stocks; comedy hosted by Katie

Mulgrew; storytelling sessions for young children in the Story Den; and dance by Everything Human Rights. In terms of theatre, the Den featured performances by the resident acting school in Spinners Mill, *A Will and a Way*, and the self-declared longest-running amateur theatre company in Britain, St Joseph's Players; rehearsed readings of the eight winning plays in the LocalTale competition (Mary Berry's *Green Leaves*, Amy Drake's *Hope is a Flower*, Lumen Hirata-Smith's *Childminding*, Charlotte Kirton's *The Tree From You or Me*, Pegeen Murphy's *Dreams for our Daughters*, Alison Ormrod's *Battery Low*, Tom Stock's *On the Streets of Covid*, Sarah Teale's *25 & Over*); KIT Theatre's *Digital Ghost Hunt*; *Our Place* – a children's production which followed a week-long drama course at Spinners Mill with young people from Leigh; Gary Lagden's play *Fly Half*, with songs written and composed by Gary Moulton; the premiere reading of Kieran Knowles' play *Some People Feel the Rain*; and Lauryn Redding's *Bloody Elle: The Gig*, an adaptation of *Bloody Elle* which reopened the Royal Exchange Theatre in June 2021. A strong regional identity was at the core of many of these performances, expressing pride for the town of Leigh, the North, and post-industrial towns in general. This distinct sense of place is captured, for example, in Lagden's *Fly Half*, which tells the story of a rugby-playing steel worker from a town in South Wales, and Redding's *Bloody Elle: The Gig* – a queer love story told from the perspective of a working class woman living in a town in the North of England.

One of the plays that was commissioned for the Den in Leigh, Knowles' *Some People Feel the Rain*, is illustrative of the Royal Exchange's methods of working across the city-region. This play, which has its premiere rehearsed reading at Spinners Mill, captures both the Royal Exchange's reputation for developing new writing and the city-town connections brought to the heart of the theatre via the Local Exchange programme. Knowles is an actor and playwright who is from Leigh, and he was commissioned by the Royal Exchange to write a play about his hometown.[4] Like many other young creatives, he left Leigh as a young adult to pursue an acting and writing career in London where he studied at LAMDA. Knowles was already networked into the Royal Exchange Theatre: the Co-Artistic Director, Bryony Shanahan, directed two of his plays, *Operation Crucible* (Sheffield Crucible, 2018 and 2021) and *Chicken Soup* (Sheffield Crucible, 2018), which emphasises the way that this city-town exchange aims to support regional cultural ecologies. The casting of *Some People Feel the Rain* also evidences these city-town connections, highlighting how artists and actors move between city and town as cultural workers.

Ntombizodwa Ndlovu, who played Jo in *Some People Feel the Rain* in Leigh in August 2021, went on to play the lead role of Camae in Roy Alexander Weise's revival of Katori Hall's *The Mountaintop* at the Royal Exchange Theatre in October 2021.

Cutting through Knowles' work is a care and attention to working class communities in England's regions, whose stories tend not to take centre stage in metropolitan networks of theatre production and curation. This is clear in his earlier plays. *Chicken Soup*, for example, details the lives of a group of women who set up a soup kitchen in Rotherham during the Miner's Strike in 1984 and still run it thirty-two years later. Knowles' interest in post-industrial communities is captured again in *Some People Feel the Rain,* which in many ways set the tone for the Den in Leigh: the torrential rain that features in the play matched the August storms during this two-week residency which posed real threats to the Den's timber structure (and led to an impromptu move of the third night of the production into the Mill's Music Centre, when a crack was discovered in one of the Den's support frames). The play is set in a family home in an unnamed town in the North of England where prolonged rainfall is wreaking havoc. While the play is about loss in an ecological sense – in that the town in the play is in danger of literally being washed away – it is also about the impact of the loss of social and economic practices associated with its industry. What is striking about the play is its focus on intergenerational relationships among women: representations of working class labour tend to be masculine in their configuration but the focus rests on the women in Knowles' play, who are supporting each other in the best way that they can. Despite this, the play's ending figures as a love letter to post-industrial towns:

> *These streets roared once*
> *They did. Once.*
>
> *Mills and factories. Pits and pubs.*
> *It's come and gone. It comes and goes*
>   (Knowles, 2021, p. 93).

As I will show, the legacies of industrial labour that hum in the background of *Some People Feel the Rain*, or as Gordon would put it, the 'social hauntings', shape every aspect of the *Digital Ghost Hunt*: the story of Spinners Mill structures the narrative of the performance, and the production is grafted to the material place of the mill itself. Contrary to Kathleen Stewart's view outlined in *The Space at the Side of the Road* that post-industrial spaces are characterised by 'a logic of negation' (1996, 17), I take the view that these industrial legacies, these 'social hauntings', provide – in Raymond Williams' terms – 'resources of hope' for townspeople (Williams, 1988). My analysis of *Digital Ghost Hunt* specifically examines how the mill's history provided an educational resource in the making of KIT Theatre's immersive production for Leigh's next generation.

Leigh and material histories of exchange

Digital Ghost Hunt mined the material exchanges that shaped the history of the mill and the town that it is located in. The show premiered at the Den at Spinners Mill, one of the few remaining double cotton mills in this former mill town. At the height of the industrial revolution, Leigh was a hub of economic exchange, with strong links to the city of Manchester via rail and canal due to its textile industries. The first major mill to open in Leigh was Bedford New Mills in 1837, and, by 1911, Leigh was the fifth largest spinning centre in Greater Manchester (Lunn, 1958, p. 261). The cotton industry in the town boomed following the expansion of canal networks to Leigh (via the extension of the Bridgewater Canal to Leigh in 1795 and its linkage with the Leeds and Liverpool Canal at Wigan in 1819) and the opening of the Liverpool and Manchester Railway in 1830 (Hall, 2001, p. 72). In addition to this movement of goods from town to city, silk and cotton production in Leigh also took place within the home. This was due to the domestic putting-out system which meant that labour was subcontracted to the houses of workers. While this practice was more common in the early stages of the region's industrial growth, it continued long into the nineteenth century. In this way, the industry had inter- and intra- town connections, working from city to town, town to town, town to village, house to house, and back again. Leigh was also a mining town, meaning that it was networked to surrounding villages and other nearby towns through its collieries. Together, working in what was known as a 'pit and mill' economy, these industries enabled greater productivity in the town and across the region. People from Leigh, known locally as 'Leithers', describe it as a town of 'coal, cotton, and canals', making clear the material practices of exchange that made it. This saying captures the historic connectivity in the town to the city and surrounding villages: if you mapped Leigh's histories of material exchange in the nineteenth and twentieth centuries, in particular, you would find a well-connected town – a key muscle of Manchester's industrial machine.

However, it is important to highlight the colonial history that underpinned Leigh's industries. The cotton industry which made the town meant that it was not only connected to the city as its primary trader, it was networked globally into the economic structures of the British Empire. Raw cotton, which was grown by enslaved people on plantations in Southern US states, such as Louisiana, Alabama, and Mississippi, was imported through the Port of Liverpool, tying this Lancashire mill town to Britain's involvement in the transatlantic slave trade (Alcott, 2007). Despite the 1833 Slavery Abolition Act which banned chattel slavery in British Colonies (with the notable exception of India), businesses in Leigh (such as Jones Brothers Company, who owned Bedford New Mills) – as with many other mill towns across Lancashire, which, as a region, was most dependent on American cotton – continued to trade with plantations in the US, profiting from goods produced by enslaved people (Holcroft, 2003, p. 11).

Returning to Gordon's hauntological method – a way of looking that is characterised by presences and absences – the colonial connections that enabled industrial growth in Greater Manchester are largely absent from the historical record. The idea that these histories of colonial violence figure as spectres, lingering in the background of dominant historical narratives on the Industrial Revolution, is captured by David Olusoga, who writes that 'the black men and women of the American South' are all too often 'the missing persons of the popular retelling of our industrial heritage' (Olusoga, 2016, p. 26). Taking inspiration from Gordon to 'confront ghostly aspects' – to look for the signals amid the traffic – I suggest that Leigh, and other Lancashire mill towns, are doubly ghosted by their former industries and the colonial practices that forged them.

While haunting is a framework which is often evoked in the context of post-industrial landscapes, these studies rarely acknowledge the legacies of chattel slavery and other forms of colonial violence that underpinned those industries. Early studies on post-industrial lifescapes focused on what Cowie and Heathcott term 'body count' which addressed the direct impact of job losses and material changes to former industrial landscapes (Cowie and Heathcott, 2003, p. 5). Yet the bodies in question were white bodies: scholars of post-industrial towns are yet to address the experiences of Black or Brown industrial workers in England at this time. Noting this lack of representation in the discipline, Jay Emery (2019) suggests that South Asian workers in textile factories in Leicester and Loughborough, African-Caribbean miners in urban collieries surrounding Nottingham, and the multi-racial industrial enclave of Butetown in Cardiff might be productive starting points for future research.[5] Working class studies are also yet to explore the 'body count' of enslaved people in the US that funded the cotton and coal industries in England in the first place. Despite this clear omission of Black and Brown people from post-industrial histories – who Olusoga refers to as 'missing persons' from English industrial heritage – the idea of ghosting has ironically been a key critical framework in these studies. This mechanism of haunting governs new work on post-industrial towns, with Sherry Linkon (2018) writing of a 'half-life' of post-industrial communities in the US and Geoff Bright (2018) applying Gordon's theory of 'social haunting' to his ethnographic practice in English coalfields. If, as Gordon argues, a haunted ontology looks for what is missing from sociological commentaries – she writes that 'to study social life, one must confront the ghostly aspects of it' – I argue here that there is an urgent demand for a decolonial approach to post-industrial landscapes. Such an approach would explore the experiences of Black and Brown industrial workers that have been thus far marginalised from the historical record and reveal the colonial connections that funded those industries.

Leigh, like other mill towns in Lancashire at the time, was conscious of its connections to enslaved Africans in the Southern states of the US. During the cotton famine from 1861 to 1864, the town's newspapers, the *Leigh Journal* and the *Leigh Chronicle*, reported widely on the American Civil War. Local support and solidarity for enslaved people across the Atlantic was captured in the establishment of the Leigh Ladies Anti-Slavery Committee, which organised a collection to donate to the pro-abolitionist cause and held a number of rallies, including one with leading abolitionist George Thompson in October 1861. Similarly in April 1862, the Leigh branch of Union and Emancipation held a meeting in Leigh Town Hall, where the speakers included a local mill owner, Caleb Wright; Peter Sinclair, who had just returned from five years travelling in the US for the abolitionist cause; and W.E. Jackson, an escaped slave. According to the *Leigh Chronicle*, these men were received warmly and the audience 'frequently manifested their applause in the warmest manner' (*Leigh Chronicle* cited in Holcroft, 2003, p. 10). That said, there were limits to the town's solidarity, and these limits raise important questions about the ways that colonial frameworks reveal themselves in visceral form, especially in times of crisis. In 1862, the Leigh Ladies Anti-Slavery annual collection was foregone in the face of extreme rises in poverty among cotton workers at home. They note that 'While thanking the friends of the slave in this district, for their liberal subscriptions last year; we may inform them, that in consideration of the distress into which our factory operatives are plunged [...] we have concluded to omit making our usual collection this year, though we feel fully sensible that that money is much needed by American Abolitionists' (Leigh Ladies Anti-Slavery Committee Annual Report, 1862).

As Eric Williams writes in his 1944 book *Capitalism and Slavery* 'it was the tremendous dependence on the triangular trade that made Manchester' (Williams, 2022, p. 68). The city's participation in the transatlantic slave trade is written right into the Royal Exchange's theatre building which is at the heart of the city. The Great Hall, where the in-the-round 'spaceship' theatre is erected, was one of the world's centres for cotton trade and the trading boards remain visible on the ceiling. Under the directorship of Bryony Shanahan and Roy Alexander Weise, the theatre is looking into the colonial legacy of its building via the Disrvpt programme which is comprised of 'riotous curated events which invite individuals or companies from a range of communities and art forms to take ownership of the Royal Exchange Theatre's Great Hall' (Royal Exchange Theatre website, 2022). The inaugural Disrvpt event, titled 'Holding Space', was created by Mancunian artist Keisha Thompson and designed by Alison Erika Forde. The piece was a poem and installation that asked questions about the Royal Exchange building, its history, and its relationship to the transatlantic slave trade, with the aim of bringing 'overlooked stories to the foreground' (Royal Exchange Theatre Disrvpt webpage, 2022). This emphasis on drilling deep into the site of the building to explore its legacies is a similar approach taken to KIT theatre with the *Digital Ghost Hunt* and evokes the same mechanisms of haunting that structure this chapter.

As the name of Thompson's installation makes clear, theatre and performance – as live, place-making media – *hold* audiences in a space in which they can work through collective, and indeed difficult, memories and histories together. Returning to Olusoga's note of the absented Black bodies, there is potential for theatre and performance to hold audiences in place and raise its ghosts. This idea that performance has the ability to raise ghosts from everyday life is explored at length by theatre academic and practitioner, Mike Pearson, in *Marking Time: Performance, Archaeology, and the City*. Pearson identifies the way that performance can tamper with everyday rhythms using Cardiff as his case study, a city which he argues is 'indelibly marked – haunted even – by the Butes' – the family who brought power and prosperity to the city through exporting coal (Pearson, 2013, p. 5). Notably, Pearson's focus is on how the Butes' legacy is visible in the contemporary configuration of the city, and he is attentive to the ways in which performance can spring up and intercept the traffic on its streets. Looking back to the radical theatre scene in Cardiff in the 1970s – which included theatre companies such as Moving Being who were based at Chapter Arts Centre (1971–) – he suggests that this work drew attention to the transport systems in the city's topography which he describes as 'composed of circulatory dynamics, mobilities and rhythms, of barely discernible temporalities and manifold narratives' (2013, pp. 8–9). Pearson's approach thus chimes with the one taken here: he reads performance practice through the histories of material exchange that shaped the city. Taking Pearson's view that performance can ask questions of a place – asking 'what happens here; has happened here; might happen here?' – I now explore the ways that KIT theatre's *Digital Ghost Hunt* traces Leigh's historic connections to the city and works to exorcise its ghosts (2013, p. 246).

Raising the ghosts: KIT Theatre's *Digital Ghost Hunt*

First developed in 2017, KIT Theatre's *Digital Ghost Hunt* is part of the company's Adventures in Learning programme which seeks to blend live performance and game mechanics to enhance creativity in schoolchildren. The programme first began ten years ago and so far, 15, 000 children have taken part in a range of settings, including schools, museums, and libraries. Made in collaboration with the King's Digital Lab and supported by Arts Council England, Heritage Lottery Funding, and the Paul Hamlyn Foundation, the *Digital Ghost Hunt* is described on KIT theatre's website as 'a ground-breaking fusion of augmented reality, coding education and immersive theatre' (KIT theatre website, 2022). The show has been adapted to a range of heritage sites across England since its creation – including York Theatre Royal and the Garden Museum in London – and it won the 2019 Digital Humanities Award in the 'Fun' category and featured in the Immersive Arcade's Best of British since 2001. In conversation with Leigh Ambassador, Mike Burwin, on the *Connecting Tales* podcast, which was made at the Den, Tom Bowtell, KIT Theatre's Artistic Director, claims that the primary aim of the *Digital Ghost Hunt* is to create a model which is suitable for 'moving across the country and haunting historic heritage spaces' in order to 'bring to life to the stories of those past places' (Local Exchange website, 2021).

The process began with Bowtell and Elliott Hall, the co-creator of *Digital Ghost Hunt*, visiting the mill and meeting the volunteers who shared stories of the space to build the narrative. Returning to the keyword 'exchange' that I have drawn on throughout this chapter, the making of the show mobilised these connections between KIT theatre – a city-based immersive theatre company – and the volunteers who have been restoring Spinners Mill in the town. These city-town connections were also brought out in the casting of the production where three of the Local Exchange Ambassadors – who are also volunteers in the Mill – played a role in the show. Mike, the interviewer for the podcast *Connecting Tales*, played Stanley the ghost, while Elizabeth Costello and Lisa Michelle shared the role of one of the workers in the building. The story (sourced from the volunteers) that stuck was that of a former mill worker who sustained injuries when the engine exploded in 1920, which inspired the creation of the character of Stanley in KIT theatre's production. The performance was thus thoroughly site-specific, taking and adapting historical events that occurred in the mill as its main narrative. According to Pearson and Michael Shanks, site-specific work can be defined as performances that are not just about the places in which they are set but are 'conceived for' and 'mounted within' them (Pearson and Shanks, 2001, p. 23). Here, Pearson and Shanks emphasise the embeddedness of these performances, noting that their site-specificity marks a meshing together of the site's 'then and there' and the audience's 'here and now' (2001, p. 25). As the *Digital Ghost Hunt* led its audiences through the spaces of the mill, it called on the historical depth of that building and brought its ghosts literally into full view. While Pearson and Shanks note that site-specific performances often work to unite past and present – bringing the 'then and there' into the 'here and now' – the *Digital Ghost Hunt* was also concerned with future optics given the educational element to this show which utilises the latest gaming technologies to work with the next generation. KIT theatre's use of the digital also chimes with the proposed plans for Mill 2 of Spinners Mill. As I noted earlier in this chapter, Spinners Mill aims to renovate the second mill into a training centre, providing professional apprenticeships and other forms of technical education which are focused on digital industries.

As Bowtell explains, the narrative of each *Digital Ghost Hunt* production is unique to the space that it is performed in and can be loosely defined as what he calls 'authentic historical fiction' (Local Exchange website 2021). While the production was in Pearson's and Shanks' terms, 'conceived for' and 'mounted within' Spinners Mill, Stanley's story was exaggerated for dramatic effect, with KIT theatre claiming that their protagonist was killed in this explosion. To meet the premise of each show – which is to 'find a ghost, help a ghost, and set a ghost free' – it becomes clear that Stanley is haunting Spinners

Mill because he has been wronged. The children soon find out that Stanley was maligned for being allegedly under the influence of alcohol when operating the machinery, and their task is to find the truth of the circumstances surrounding his death. In this way, *Digital Ghost Hunt* is a social haunting writ large. Returning to Gordon's idea that 'the ghost always carries the message', it is clear that this is played out literally in the production with the character of Stanley who takes the audience on a journey through the mill to clear his name (Gordon, 2008, p. 98). The message that Stanley carries is centred on seeking justice for the worker and working collectively to prove his innocence, highlighting how KIT theatre taps into the wider narratives relating to Leigh's industrial history as a strong union town. Yet, there is also a missed opportunity here, a space in which the children could learn a more diversely and richly constituted history of their town. Given the progressive aesthetic of the show – where the children were encouraged to think through and debate issues of justice and fairness – there is potential here to expand the frame of reference to include the legacies of harm that enabled Leigh's industries: the ghosts of the enslaved people in the American South.

Digital Ghost Hunt further draws on the town's histories of making through its style of production. Here, KIT theatre harnesses the industrial legacies of not only the town but also the building itself, using the past, in Williams' terms, as a 'resource of hope' for the future. In his discussion of former mining communities in South Wales, Williams pinpoints this hope specifically to 'resources of class and community' (Williams, 1988, p. 97). In doing so, he notes that post-industrial landscapes can be defined as places 'where generations of not only economic but of social effort and human care have been invested, and which new generations will inherit' (1988, p. 124). These resources of collective social capital are clearly animated in the *Digital Ghost Hunt*, where the children work together to help the wronged worker. In line with Leigh's history as a textile town, the performance engages the children using tactile codes, meaning that they interact with this heritage site by walking through its spaces, smelling the hot oil of the engine room, and touching cogs and sprockets that are scattered around the mill.

This emphasis on doing and making is made clear from the beginning of the production where each child is given a handheld device which can detect a 'ghostly' presence in that material. Designed by Hall, the handheld ghost detectors are made from two microcomputers which enable the children to identify objects that have been 'touched' by a ghost. The detectors each pick up different traces – left in ultraviolet paint or ectoplasm – which means that the children need

Made to Connect 111

to work collectively to piece together a full picture and solve the mystery. This outlines the agency given to the children and means that no show was the same: the actors – in the roles of Professor Bray and Deputy Undersecretary Quill – encouraged the children (and their parents) to respond to the material in their own way rather than following a scaffolded production narrative. Returning to Pearson's note on the potential of site-specific theatre to hold audiences collectively in place, the semi-structured production opens a space for the children to creatively imagine, in Pearson's terms, 'what happens here; has happened here; might happen here?' (Pearson, 2013, p. 246). This semi-improvised quality is clear in the fact that the ghost hunt is not scripted, it is loosely structured around the placement of the objects in the building which led the children to Stanley.

Quill instructs the children to look for 'truth in junk', making clear the counter-hegemonic impulse of the production. Rather than viewing the cogs and springs as debris to be cast aside, these scraps provide the clues to enable the children to piece together what really happened to Stanley. Notably, the evidence of the mill manager's neglect – including the faulty engine parts and the whisky bottle that he planted in Stanley's locker – is authentic historical material. These props are unique to this site as they were sourced directly from Spinners Mill's Heritage Centre, which is open to the public several days a week and host to local schools. Going back to Gordon's original definition of social hauntings, the historical objects are material traces of the mill's industrial history, and, when placed in this production setting, they serve as disruptive 'reminders' of past social violence, of the closure of those industries. In picking up and sorting through piles of cogs and chains, the audience engages with the materiality of the mill and the remnants of its industry are warm in the hands of the children.

This tactile journey through Spinners Mill is sustained right to the end of the production. After finding the letters that were stuffed in Mr. Fitzherbert's desk and revealing their contents in invisible ink which expressed Stanley's concerns about the engine, the real story of his death is complete. Gathered in the engine room, the children are then invited to tell this story in their own way. On the company's website, KIT theatre asserts that its aim is 'to make playful, immersive theatre for, by and with young people which improves their relationship to learning and develops their empathy, resilience and critical thinking' (KIT theatre website, 2022). Empathy and critical thinking ran through every aspect of *Digital Ghost Hunt* but was especially marked in these closing moments. Together, the children are tasked with deciding the best way to capture in writing what happened to Stanley, and they rewrite the report in their own words. This highlights the show's progressive aesthetic: the children from this post-industrial town are given the agency to right the historical record, literally writing the 'truth' of an event that occurred in this building on its walls. In the production that I saw, the children's empathy with the wronged worker was also particularly resonant as one child cried out 'we love you, Stanley!' as the ghost disappeared from view.

Conclusion

Working across the Greater Manchester region and in place at Spinners Mill, the Local Exchange programme enabled two city-based theatre companies, KIT theatre and the Royal Exchange Theatre, to create a place-based production where local children could explore the rich histories of connection in this heritage site that remains at the heart of their town. Through animating Spinners Mill, *Digital Ghost Hunt* made clear theatre's ability to disrupt the rhythms of everyday spaces and bring out the residual traces of the past within the townscape through creative practice. As the children moved around the spaces of the mill, looking for 'truth in junk' and working collectively to help the wronged worker, they fostered the kind of collective social capital that defined the town in its industrial prime. Despite the closure of its industries, these legacies of collective social capital persist and the very presence of Spinners Mill in 2022 – and its centrality to cultural practice in Leigh moving forward – stand as stubborn reminders of the town's industrial heritage, signalling the way that the past figures in Williams' terms as a 'resource of hope', as fuel, for the future cultural life of this post-industrial town.

Yet the progressive aesthetic of *Digital Ghost Hunt* is also quietly radical. Contrary to the newness of the townscape where retail outlets have been built on former mill grounds, the production looks to the town's industrial past, with Quill reminding the audience that 'we're here because this area is under siege from ghostly hauntings' (KIT theatre, 2021, p. 5). Indeed, the town is besieged by its industrial legacies and my contention here is that Leigh, and other post-industrial towns, should attend to its ghosts, rather than try to shake them. The ghosts of the town's industrial past are marked into the landscape – in the mills, headstocks, and civic buildings – and, to borrow Walter Benjamin's words that Gordon cites in *Ghostly Matters*, these material traces serve as reminders that things 'could have been and could be otherwise' (Benjamin cited in Gordon, 2008, p. 57). It is in this counter-hegemonic register that there is potential in the form of

Digital Ghost Hunt to open up some of the lesser-known histories of Leigh and other mill towns in the North of England, including the region's dependency on slave-grown cotton. Not only does the production 'raise ghosts', it asks children to look for alternative histories and knowledges that slight the historical record, cultivating a way of looking that could change the way we think about civic performance cultures in towns. Quill's instruction to help not fear ghosts offers an inspirational model for future cultural practice in post-industrial towns, one which attends to the complexity of past and present cultural ecologies and moves towards a more richly constituted history of these places in the future.

Notes

1 The plan for the second mill – which is yet to be restored – is centred on developing technical education opportunities. This next project aims to address the fact that there is currently no post-16 provision in Leigh, with students having to travel to Wigan or Salford to attend college. Emphasis will be placed here on digital opportunities which chimes with the previous work of Spinners Mill's general manager, Jo Platt. As the former Labour MP for Leigh (2017–2019), Platt was also promoted to Shadow Minister for the Cabinet Office where she called for a growth in the cyber sector in post-industrial towns.
2 Despite being neighbouring towns, there is a long history of rivalry between Wigan and Leigh. As they are now in the same borough, Wigan and Leigh are often referred to as a pair, rather than separate towns with distinct identities which disgruntles residents in both towns.
3 For more information on the British Drama League and its influence on the National Theatre, see: Jane Milling with Helen Nicholson and Nadine Holdsworth, 'Valuing Amateur Theatre' in *The Ecologies of Amateur Theatre*.
4 Knowles writes about this experience and on the themes of (dis)connection that structure this chapter in his blog for the Royal Exchange Theatre and the Bruntwood Prize (Knowles 2021).
5 This work is already being undertaken at a community level. See, for example, the Black Miners Museum which details the experiences of Black coal miners around Nottingham (Black Miners Museum website, 2022).

Bibliography

Alcott, W. (2007). How money from slavery made Greater Manchester. Available at http://revealinghistories.org.uk/how-did-money-from-slavery-help-develop-greater-manchester/articles/the-rise-of-capitalism-and-the-development-of-europe.html (Accessed 13 June 2022).

Arts Council England website. Available at: https://www.artscouncil.org.uk/LUCPs#section-1 (Accessed 13 June 2022).

Black Miners Museum website. (2022). Available at: https://www.blackcoalminers.com (Accessed 12 May 2022).
Bright, G. (2018). Working with Social Haunting website. Available at: https://www.socialhaunting.com (Accessed 28 March 2022).
Cowie, J. and Heathcott, J. (2003). *Beyond the Ruins: The Meanings of Deindustrialisation*. New York: Cornell University Press.
Emery, J. (2019). 'Geographies of Deindustrialisation and the Working Class: Industrial Ruination, Legacies and affect', *Geography Compass*, 13(2), e12417. Available at: https://compass.onlinelibrary.wiley.com/doi/10.1111/gec3.12417 (Accessed 12 June 2022).
Gordon, A. (2008). *Ghostly Matters: Haunting and the Sociological Imagination*. Minnesota: University of Minnesota Press.
Hall, N. (2001). 'The Emergence of the Liverpool Raw Cotton Market, 1800–1850,' *Northern History*, 38(1), pp. 65–81.
Hirst, I. (2021). Interview with Gemma Edwards for Civic Theatres: A Place for Towns (AHRC).
HM Government. (2022). 'Levelling Up the United Kingdom'. Crown Copyright.
Holcroft, F. (2003). *The Lancashire Cotton Famine Around Leigh*. Leigh: Leigh Local History Society.
KIT Theatre. (2021). *Digital Ghost Hunt: Leigh Spinners Mill*. Unpublished script.
KIT Theatre website. (2022). Available at: https://www.kittheatre.org (Accessed 21 March 2022.
Knowles, K. (2021). *Some People Feel the Rain*. Unpublished script.
Knowles, K. (2021). 'Kieran Knowles: Leigh and Some People Feel the Rain'. Available at: https://www.writeaplay.co.uk/kieran-knowles-blog-wed-11th-august/ (Accessed 21 May 2022.
Leigh Ladies Anti-Slavery Committee Annual Report. (1862). Held at Leigh Local Studies archive. Reference: Vootson Collection 326.
Leigh Spinners Mill website. (2022). Available at: https://www.leighspinnersmill.co.uk (Accessed 13 June 2022).
Linkon, S. (2018). *The Half-Life of Deindustrialization: Working-Class Writing About Economic Restructuring*. Ann Arbor: The University of Michigan Press.
Local Exchange Theatre website. (2021). Available at: https://www.royalexchange.co.uk/local-exchange (Accessed 21 March 2022).
Lunn, J. (1958). *History of Leigh*. Manchester: P & D Riley.
Milling, J, Nicholson, H and Holdsworth, N. (2018). 'Valuing Amateur Theatre' in Nicholson, H, Holdsworth, N and Milling, Jane. (eds.), *The Ecologies of Amateur Theatre*. Basingstoke: Palgrave Macmillan, pp. 23–65.
Olusoga, D. (2016). *Black and British: A Forgotten History*. London: Picador.
Pearson, M. (2013). *Marking Time: Performance, Archaeology and the City*. Exeter: University of Exeter Press.
Pearson, M. and Shanks, M. (2001). *Theatre Archaeology: Disciplinary Dialogues*. London: Routledge.
Public Works website. (2022). Available at: https://publictheater.org/programs/publicworks/ (Accessed 28 June 2022).

Royal Exchange Theatre Disrvpt webpage. (2022). Available at: https://www.royalexchange.co.uk/disrvpt (Accessed 13 June 2022).
Royal Exchange Theatre website. (2022). Available at: https://www.royalexchange.co.uk (Accessed 21 March 2022).
Stewart, K. (1996). *A Space on the Side of the Road: Cultural Poetics in an 'Other' America*. Princeton: Princeton University Press.
Trueman, M. (2018). 'Why rural life is theatreland's hot topic and how Brexit played a part', *The Telegraph*. Available at: https://www.telegraph.co.uk/theatre/what-to-see/whyrural-life-now-theatrelands-hot-topic-brexit-has-played/ (Accessed 28 March 2022).
Williams, E. (2022). *Capitalism and Slavery*. London: Penguin Classics.
Williams, R. (1988). *Resources of Hope: Culture, Democracy, Socialism*. London: Verso.

6 Hopeful Futures
Theatres in Towns

Gemma Edwards and Cara Gray

It is an evening in November 2021 and we are huddled in Heena Fabrics, a textile shop, in Deeplish, Rochdale, participating in a walking performance, *Stories We Tell*. Fabrics are brushing our shoulders and there is audio-visual footage being projected on the cloth that is draped on the walls. Behind us, a man is working in a side room: he is quietly undertaking his labour, working the fabrics with his hands. On the walls, a video is being screened, and it shows several local people speaking about what this shop means to them. One speaker is Rochdale-based creative facilitator, Bushra Sultana, who recalls how she used to visit the shop with friends and family, playing upstairs surrounded by the stock while her mother pored over the best fabric. The shop, gradually transformed now as graphics are projected onto its walls, has thrived under the ownership of Heena for over thirty years: it is always busy, and, for many generations of families in Deeplish, it is a landmark of home.

Stories We Tell was an audio walking tour directed by Parvez Qadir, a writer and director from Rochdale, conceived as a way to celebrate his hometown. As director of arts organisation, Breaking Barriers, Qadir works alongside communities in place to tell their stories using a range of art forms, including audio, soundscapes, film, and animation. The project, first shown in October 2021, was funded by Touchstones Museum in Rochdale and Manchester Independents, a special funding scheme set up to support freelance artists during the global pandemic. As one of the most diverse neighbourhoods in the UK – around 50 languages are spoken just in this one part of town – this site-specific production aimed to capture, and share, what home means to people living in Deeplish and Milkstone today. Beginning by the train station, the tour animated the streets, with its audience viewing snippets of videos being screened from the windows of a front room of a terraced house, on the brick walls of a children's playpark

DOI: 10.4324/9781003308058-6

by the local mosque, and finishing up in the Community Centre where hot cups of tea, jalebi, and chips and chutney were shared. Marketed as 'a love letter to Rochdale', this performance was just that – drawing attention to the place and people of Deeplish and Milkstone and literally splashing stories on its pavements, walls, houses, and shops.

In the same month, over 200 miles from Rochdale in Letchworth Garden City, Hertfordshire, the Settlement Players welcomed audiences back into their theatre for the first time in over a year and a half with a production of Noel Coward's 1939 play *Present Laughter*. The Settlement Players are an amateur theatre company who have been part of Letchworth's theatre scene since 1923, taking their name from Letchworth Settlement, an independent adult education centre, where the group first formed.[1] Today, the Settlement is housed in an Arts and Crafts style former temperance inn – once named The Skittles Inn – which used to act as a meeting place for the town's early residents, hosting progressive societies, trade union meetings, dances, and lectures. As the Settlement, it remains an important meeting place in the town today, running a varied programme of practical and educational classes and workshops across arts, crafts, languages, creative writing, and special interest subjects alongside being home to many of the town's groups and societies. The Players continue to meet, make, rehearse, and perform theatre at the Settlement. On Sunday mornings, the centre's multi-purpose hall is transformed into a set building workshop where scenery is painted and sets are assembled. Meanwhile, during the Players' three productions a year (plus a handful of one-act plays), the 'Little Theatre' is brought to life in the hall: rows of stackable chairs are laid out in front of the stage to create an auditorium, while collapsible tables and trolleys create a bar, box office, and lighting and sound decks.

Letchworth Settlement's centenary year was 2020, but celebrations had to be put on hold as the centre faced an uncertain future due to Covid-19 lockdown measures leading to financial difficulties. News of its potential permanent closure was met by local support in the form of money, time, and ideas. A crowdfunding campaign 'Save our Settlement' raised money through donations from the town's residents, including the Settlement Players who donated by doubling their rent. Meanwhile, innovative ideas about how to save the centre were offered through newly formed (and now ongoing) partnerships with local organisations, including the Letchworth Leisure and Arts Group – a volunteer-led, non-profit organisation that promotes, supports, and connects people with local arts and leisure groups in the town – who worked with the Settlement to organise a series of concerts by young musicians, with ticket sales and performance fees acting as donations to save the building. These efforts successfully helped to save the centre from closure, and in doing so, secured a certain future for the Settlement Players' Little Theatre.

These stories evidence the multiple ways that theatre – as event, company, and venue – sits within cultural, civic, and commercial spaces and networks in English towns. As we have explored over the course of this book, performance in towns happens in a range of places: in a grade II listed double cotton mill, an old court room, corn exchange, malt house, renovated stables, a park, a fabric shop, and on the street. At the same time, theatre buildings in towns serve their communities in a range of ways, hosting playgroups and other activities for children, offering training and workshops to teenagers, facilitating adult education programmes, providing coffee mornings for the elderly, and supporting small local businesses through farmers' markets and craft sales. This multi-functionality means that theatres in towns are versatile: not only do they play a key role in community-making (social life), but they can also boost night-time economies (economic life) in addition to preserving and restoring existing buildings (material life). Theatre's potential environmental imperative – its capacity to save historic buildings via sustainable restoration practices – has been given new emphasis by the recent publication of the Theatres Trust's *Theatre Green Book* (2021) which suggests that renovating old buildings (instead of building new ones) is 'the most sustainable thing we can do' (Theatres Trust, 2021). In short, then, the practice of theatre in towns is not confined to theatre buildings, and purpose-built theatre buildings are host to many other activities which extend beyond the practice of theatre.

This versatility, the ability to adapt and transform to meet the needs of a place and the people that live there, is facilitated by the scale of towns, as we briefly noted in the introduction to this book. Smaller than cities but larger than villages, towns can be understood as places that support social experiment and innovation. In each chapter, we have seen experiment and innovation play out in different ways, responding to specific townscapes and histories and the diverse performance practices – and wider cultural ecologies – that shape them. In Chapter 2, Nicholson explores how theatres in towns contribute to a hopeful vision of what it means to be local, while in Chapter 3, Hughes looks at an experimental model of cultural co-production in Wigan which establishes a new touring network across towns and cities nationally, and intersects with an innovative approach to community-wealth building in the borough. In Chapter 4, Gray follows how a volunteer-led amateur theatre is becoming a space of hybridity: inviting new people, ideas, audiences, and ways of working that complicate the distinctions between amateur and professional theatres and theatre-making. In Chapter 5, Edwards explores city-town exchanges, focusing specifically on the ways that contemporary cultural practice in post-industrial towns can mine the legacies of production that made those places to shape the future. This chapter takes forward the idea that a town's histories, its ghosts, can provide in Raymond Williams' terms 'resources of hope' for future generations (Williams, 1989, p. 1). Here, we develop our discussion of experiment, which, in turn, ensures that the imaginative potential of towns is emphasised in the closing notes of the book. In doing so, we understand the idea of hope as threaded through the past, present, and future temporalities of towns – and this chapter aims to begin to trace those lines of historical connection.

The histories of the two towns featuring in the opening of this chapter show the significance of social experiment, as well as its potential to function as models for future practice in radical and sustainable town planning: Rochdale, the birthplace of the cooperative movement, and Letchworth, the original Garden City. In 1844, eight working class men, who would later become known as the Rochdale Pioneers, opened the first cooperative shop at 31 Toad Lane, Rochdale – just under a mile from Station Road where Breaking Barriers' *Stories We Tell* began. The cooperative movement, now international in its scale, originated in this mill town in Greater Manchester following bouts of high unemployment, hunger, and the failure of the Chartist movement to secure political enfranchisement for working men. In this way, crisis produced experimental and radical thinking, echoing Rebecca Solnit's observation that 'Inside the word emergency is emerge, from an emergency new things come forth. The old certainties are crumbling fast, but danger and possibilities are sisters' (Solnit, 2016, p. 13). The new thing to emerge in Rochdale was a set of cooperative values that offered a radical re-imagining of the way that the market works. The cooperative movement effectively socialised the market, developing practices of collective community wealth, shared ownership, and regulated surplus. Central to this new economic logic was the desire to secure fair prices for high-quality daily goods for ordinary working people, such as butter, sugar, flour, and oatmeal. Historian Peter Gurney characterises the movement as driven by 'An ethical, idealist impulse' of cooperation that 'was seen as a way of building an alternative to capitalism from the bottom up, replacing bourgeois individualism with a society based on mutuality and social solidarity' (Gurney,

2003, 114). Placing emphasis on sharing for the common good rather than profit, the cooperative movement offered an alternative way of doing commerce in this town and beyond, and this third way has proved resilient, standing the test of time.

Rochdale's history as the birthplace of the cooperative movement is directly influencing future cultural policy in the town. This is captured in the 'Culture Co-Op' (2022–), Rochdale's successful bid to Arts Council England's Creative People Places programme, which brings together a consortium of organisations: the Co-Operative Group, Rochdale Council, the community group Action Together, Your Trust, and Rochdale Borough Housing. Taking its lead from the co-op store, one of the aims of the Culture Co-Op is to set up material shops which respond to cultural demand in that area and work with local providers to meet the needs of that place and the people who live there. The 'culture shops' are built on the premise of building a group of 'culture pioneers', a network of volunteers who co-design programmes tailored to their local area, in order to build 'culture neighbourhoods', clusters of activity that come together to make a thriving cultural ecology (Grice, 2021). This responsivity to place can be found in the methods of working captured in Gray's and Edwards' chapters where movements of meshworks and networks structure cultural activity in the coastal and post-industrial towns in question.

The New Culture Quarter in Rochdale links the cultural programme to key heritage sites in the town which have recently been renovated by Historic England's Heritage Action Zone scheme. During this research project, we have worked in several towns that are receiving High Street Heritage Action Zone funding, an important programme which is transforming town centres, including Wigan and Hastings which feature as key case studies in this book (Historic England, 2022). The first phase of regeneration in Rochdale begins at the town hall centrepiece – which is currently under renovation – moving up the road to Touchstones Museum by the college and sixth form, up Drake Street to the train station, and taking in Broadfield Park, too. As Darren Grice (Deputy Chief Executive of Your Trust [the Rochdale Borough Cultural Trust]) highlights, there is a clear opportunity for culture to animate those civic spaces. One headline of our research has been to explore the offer that theatre and culture present in this animating role. As town centres have shifted from being places to buy things to providing things to do, theatre and performance can play with the everyday rhythms of these spaces. By working with townspeople and through performance events, theatre can experiment with and establish new quotidian tempos – a renewed sense of place, as well as imaginative and social uses – in and for these spaces. In Rochdale, Grice saw this potential in *Stories We Tell*, the site-specific piece with which we began this chapter, as well as in the 8000 km journey of Little Amal that opened this book and also included a stop in Rochdale.

While the cooperative movement was concerned with goods, the garden city movement – which first materialised in Letchworth in 1903 – applied its key principles to land ownership. In *Tomorrow: A Peaceful Path to Real Reform* (1898) – later republished as *Garden Cities of To-morrow* (1902) – Ebenezer Howard set out his utopian vision for a new kind of settlement which responded to the lack of social cohesion and overcrowded and polluted living conditions in industrial towns in England in the nineteenth century. The cooperative movement influenced the economic logic of the garden city: for Howard it 'provided a coherent framework within which to apply cooperative principles to a wide slice of local economic activity' (Town and Country Planning Association, 2021). Howard's garden city model suggested that alongside private enterprises, the core assets that support a town – including retail, utilities, leisure, land, and housing – should be in the hands of its residents. This meant that land value was retained by the community through public ownership. Profits from the core activities listed above were reinvested back into the town and its facilities; and the residents, who were shareholders in the town, had a say in how it was run, echoing the mechanisms of the dividend that was invented in Rochdale half a century earlier.

This cooperative and mutual approach was also driven by an ambition to meet human needs through a new holistic urban design approach to town planning. Calling for a union that Howard called 'Town-Country', this design brought together the best aspects of the town (sociability and access to art and entertainment) and the country (green space, clean air, and locally grown food) (Howard, 1902, p. 47). Echoing the Rochdale Pioneers of the nineteenth century, along with the cultural pioneers in Rochdale today, Letchworth had its own group of garden city pioneers – a name given to the town's early residents who were keen supporters of Howard and his proposed utopian vision. Garden city pioneers helped to shape the town in many ways. They placed emphasis on the role of arts and culture in the everyday life of Letchworth, as part of a cooperative approach to society and its wellbeing: from the many art, music, literary, and theatre societies that sprung up in the town's early days to its romantic vernacular architecture (Henderson, Lock and Ellis, 2017). Original Letchworth architects, and early residents, Barry Parker and Raymond Unwin were followers of the Arts and Crafts movement and influenced by the ideas of its leading figures John Ruskin and William Morris. Central to their design of the town was an emphasis on beautiful, practical homes that utilised sunlight and outdoor space for everyone, architecture that existed in harmony with the environment, and thoughtful planning that would aid social cohesion and connection. One example being through shared community facilities including the building that is now the Letchworth Settlement, formerly The Skittles Inn.

Today, the Town and Country Planning Association (TCPA), a group founded by Howard in 1899 to promote the idea of garden cities, are returning to and re-envisioning how the original principles set out by Howard might be resilient to towns in the twenty-first century and beyond – speaking to national and global issues including housing crises, health challenges, and a climate emergency.[2] Enduring key principles include: community ownership of land and long-term stewardship of town assets; mixed tenure and genuinely affordable healthy homes; and planning that enables access to local jobs and cultural and recreational facilities through initiatives such as 'the 20 minute neighbourhood'- a planning approach that reassesses the liveability of our towns and asks for the creation of neighbourhoods that are walkable or cyclable. Alongside these revised principles, there is also a consideration of the role that arts and culture play as part of a cooperative way of living. Today, Letchworth's lively theatre scene – expressed by the fact that there are currently four active amateur theatre groups in the town – and abundance of active arts and leisure groups and societies is indebted to its early resident pioneers.

The garden city ideals are being clearly reimagined for the twenty-first century, but the thinking underpinning these ideals also intersects with current grassroots practical experiments, or as Dobson writes 'alternative proposals', emerging in and for towns (Dobson, 2017, p. 1028). For example, national, and increasingly international, networks of groups including Transition Towns – established in Totnes in Devon in 2006 – and Incredible Edible – established in Todmorden in West Yorkshire in 2008 – are expanding with aims of tackling climate and food crises through small action at a town level.[3] Here, self-organising community groups in towns work to re-imagine their localities through participatory methods and projects. These networked methods and projects see groups caring for green spaces; creating community and educational allotments in order to re-localise food systems and provide hands-on learning; setting up community-owned renewable energy projects and companies; holding workshops and cafes where repair and DIY skills are taught; and growing food on disused plots on public land which anyone is allowed to take. Some 'Transition Towns' – including Stroud in Gloucestershire, Totnes, and Lewes in East Sussex – have even experimented with creating complimentary local currencies with the aim of encouraging a more transparent and localised economy which is captured, for example, in the Lewes Pound, although many of these currencies have not been sustainable in the long term.[4]

Practices of mutual aid can also be traced back to the principles of the Garden City and cooperative movements, and this concept was frequently mobilised by communities during the Covid-19 pandemic, giving rise to a kind of radical social care (Badger et al, 2022). Mutual aid is not a new idea, but a recycled one. First popularised by anarchist philosopher Peter Kropotkin in his 1902 essay collection 'Mutual Aid: A Factor of Evolution' – which also inspired Howard's garden city – mutual aid stresses the importance of cooperation, collaboration, and reciprocity over competition as being fundamental to human and social development. New research by Adam Badger, Philip Brown, Jennifer Cole, Matthias Kispert, and Oli Mould explores the community fridge as an example of mutual aid: a voluntary reciprocal exchange where a giver might become a receiver – and vice versa – at any point in the transaction (2022). Community fridges in our towns attend to increasing food insecurities whilst reducing the stigma that surrounds visiting food banks and registering with charities, as well as addressing concerns of overproduction and food waste.

These glimpses into the pasts and presents of Rochdale and Letchworth articulate the stories of change that potentially exist in the cultural life of many English towns and places further afield. From the Rochdale Pioneers in the mid-nineteenth century to twenty-first century practices of mutual aid, towns have themselves been theatres of social experiment in which new ideas are born and old ones are recycled and repurposed. Theatre events, companies, and venues often sit within or alongside these practical social experiments, figuring as a cultural technology for practicing new and alternative ways of living. However, it is important to note that these social experiments are rarely straightforwardly utopic. Historically, these approaches, tried and tested in English towns, have limitations, and carry complex social histories. For example, some forms of civic and cultural philanthropy in industrial towns in England in the nineteenth century were often directly funded by economic profits gleaned from colonial oppression, as Hughes and Edwards acknowledge in their chapters on Wigan and Leigh. At the same time, the garden city vision echoes the Victorian paternalism from which it took inspiration: it largely consisted of middle-class people promoting a healthy model for living to working class people. Such class inequalities continue to be played out in newer practical experiments – such as the Transition Town movement – where local, sustainable practices often depend on significant social capital, time, and resources. As Nicholson points out in Chapter 2, the term local – particularly when situated in a wider environmental discourse – is not benign either and can quickly become associated with parochial thought, as explored in Steve Hanson's study of localism and Todmorden (Hanson, 2014).

While we celebrate the hope and resilience associated with these cultural experiments, we understand the ways that these also place emphasis on the capacity of townspeople to make things work and find solutions to complex challenges, despite, in many contexts, a lack of funding. We can imagine a scenario, where, if such experiments were complemented by properly funded infrastructure for social and cultural life, they promise a very positive future for towns. In recent years, the socialisation of capital – seen in the emphasis on cooperatives, mutual aid, and land trusts – was refigured in Labour's policies on the run up to the 2019 election, constituting what some political theorists have termed 'the institutional turn' (Guinan and O'Neill, 2018). While these principles continue to be refashioned in different contexts – from small-scale experiments at neighbourhood level to Leftist party policy – they also have broad appeal across a range of political constituencies as sensible solutions to local and global challenges facing towns and townspeople. They are appearing in – and appealing to – towns of contrasting and shifting political allegiances, and, in a context of widespread distrust of formal political actors and processes, this characteristic of broad appeal encourages us to argue that such experiments provide both a shared sense of hope, and a creative and pragmatic response to crisis.

As the first study on theatre in towns, our book documents and analyses a portion of the richness and complexity of contemporary performance practice in towns, and aims to initiate further academic inquiry. While this book has focused on the English national context, a common thread which connects our chapters is the fact that theatres in towns work in wider geographic ecologies, making connections to surrounding villages and cities, and moving beyond national boundaries into global spaces. The movements that sustain these connections are clearly articulated in this book: in Gray's use of the concept of meshworks and Edwards' exploration of networks, but are also present in Hughes' discussion of queer regional diaspora – which connects Wigan to New York – and Nicholson's exploration of the global reach of the local. Drawing strength from these movements, we have explored how theatre and performance in English towns is imbricated in global, regional, and local networks of influence and materialisation.

Towns are multi-layered places – overlaying histories, activities, and ideas – and their material architectures hold the legacies of these cycles of change. In writing this book, we have visited coastal towns where seaside arcades and dodgems neighbour shiny modern art galleries, which sit in amongst fishing boats, beach huts, and hatches selling the catch of the day. We have spent time in post-industrial towns where hulking mills stand alongside late-twentieth-century shopping centres, and where theatre takes place in old warehouses flanked by grand Victorian municipal buildings. We visited a former spa resort where the theatre is the beating heart of a town surrounded by the rugged landscape of a National Park, and commuter towns where red-bricked factory blocks have been replaced with glass-walled corporate headquarters of global companies. Theatres are of course part of these rich topographies of place – acting as social hubs and sustaining creative activity locally – but theatre practice also has the capacity to animate townscapes, allowing us to experience our towns in new ways. As townspeople continue to navigate these old and new identities – tussling between old memories and new realities – theatres hold this imaginative potential, offering a place to test out and dream up alternative ways of living and doing.

Notes

1 The Letchworth Settlement was one of a number of Settlement Houses established from the late 19th century by reformers who sought to provide the working classes with access to educational courses. For more information see: letchworth.com/blog/business-blog-the-letchworth-settlement-from-1920-to-2018.
2 See for example the 'Tomorrow 125' project launched in 2023: tomorrow125.org.uk.
3 For information on both networks see: transitionnetwork.org and incredibleedible.org.uk.
4 For information on the Lewes Pound see: thelewespound.org.

Bibliography

Badger, A., Brown, P., Cole, J., Kispert, M. and Mould, O. (2022). *Manifesto for Mutual Aid*. Available at: mutualaid.uk/manifesto (Accessed 10 May 2022).

Grice, D. (2021). Interview with Jenny Hughes for Civic Theatres: A Place for Towns (AHRC).

Guinan, J. and O'Neill, M. (2018). *The institutional turn: Labour's new political economy*. Available at: https://renewal.org.uk/archive/vol-26-2018/the-institutional-turn-labours-new-political-economy/ (Accessed 7 July 2022).

Gurney, P. (2003). 'The Co-Operative Movement' in Outhwaite, W. (ed.), *The Blackwell Dictionary of Modern Social Thought*. London: Blackwell, pp. 114–116.

Hanson, S. (2014). *Small Towns, Austere Times: The Dialectic of Deracinated Localism*. London: Zero Books.

Henderson, K., Lock, K. and Ellis, H. (2017). *The Art of Building a Garden City: Designing New Communities for the 21st Century*. Newcastle upon Tyne: RIBA Publishing.

Historic England. (2022). Available at: https://historicengland.org.uk/services-skills/heritage-action-zones/ (Accessed 12 May 2022).

Howard, E. (1902). *Garden Cities of To-morrow*. London: S. Sonnenschein & Co., Ltd.

Dobson, J. (2017). 'From 'me towns' to 'we towns': Activist Citizenship in UK Town centres', *Citizenship Studies*, 21(8), pp. 1015–1033.

Solnit, R. (2016). *Hope in the Dark: Untold Histories, Wild Possibilities*. Edinburgh: Canongate Publishing.

Theatres Trust (2021). *Theatre Green Book Two: Sustainable Buildings*. Available at: https://theatregreenbook.com/book-two-sustainable-buildings/ (Accessed 13 June 2022).

Town and Country Planning Association (2021). Tomorrow 125 Interim Report. Available at: https://tcpa.org.uk/resources/tomorrow-125-interim-report/ (Accessed 12 June 2022).

Williams, R. (1989). *Resources of Hope: Culture, Democracy, Socialism*. London: Verso Books.

Index

Acott, Tim 72
Almond, Gabriel and Verba, Sidney 44
alternative town proposals 76, 122
amateur theatre 4, 9, 13, 16, 26–27, 34, 38, 66–67, 69, 77, 81, 83–88, 117, 119, 122
Appadurai, Arjun 14, 21, 22, 37
Armstrong, Stephen 42
Arts Council England 5–6, 16, 95, 100, 108; Creative People and Places *Home Slough* 22, 24–25; Levelling Up for Culture Places 95; priority places 95
austerity 5, 16, 42, 48, 51

Badger, Adam 123
Barefoot Opera 73
Battersea Arts Centre 53
belonging 7, 9, 12, 33
Berlant, Lauren, cruel optimism 44–45
Borsay, Peter 44
Breaking Barriers 116, 119
Brown, Philip 123
Bussel, Helen 66

Campbell, Beatrix 42
Casson & Friends 25
Centre for Towns 3, 7
Chakraborti, Neil 30
Chesham, Buckinghamshire, UK 8, 14, 19–21
Chesham Library 19–21; *I am a bird,* Klimis, Marie 19–21; Walters, Sally 21

Christie, Agatha 27
circular economy 6
civic amenities 1, 3
civic buildings 6
civic cultures 6, 15, 42–43, 44–45
civic institutions 1, 44, 46–47
civic pride 3
civic regeneration 43–44, 48–49, 51–52
civic role of the arts 44–45
civic spectacle 44, 48–49
civil society 15
coal mining 94, 95, 106, 113
coastal regeneration, arts and culture led regeneration 67, 69–75
coastal town (also: Seaside town) 66–69, 71–72, 75, 89
coastification 71, 75
Cobbett, William 17
Cochrane, Clare 4
co-creation 53–54
Cole, Jennifer 123
colonial legacies and histories 98, 105, 106–107
colonialism 43, 44, 46, 49–50
community 23, 26, 28–30, 36
community activities 24, 30, 31
community asset 26, 34, 76
community fridges 35, 123
community groups 120, 122
Community land trusts 76
community ownership 76, 122
community programming 16, 24
community voice 15, 25
community wealth building 51–53
community wellbeing 13, 24

community-led regeneration 75–76
Company Fierce and Quarantine, *Susan and Darren* 57
Cooperative movement (and: cooperative approach) 119–123
co-producing 22–26
Corn Exchange, Wallingford 26–36, 66; Sinodun Players, The 26, 27–28, 31, 33
cost-of-living crisis 5
Cottam, Hilary, radical help 52
cotton famine 106
cotton production 94–95, 104–106
Covid-19 2, 5, 12, 24, 33, 46, 51, 81, 94, 101–102, 117, 123
Craft town 16
creative city 4
creative economy 48, 51
cultural assets 24, 36
cultural exchange 9
cultural heritage 9
cultural participation 9, 22, 38
cultural value 2, 9, 13, 25
culture, homogenous 14, 27
culture, shared 14
culture Co-Op (Rochdale) 120
cultures, food 24
cultures, local and global 16

Davenport, Jonny 50–51
Davoudi, Simin 14, 15
Dhol Collective 25
Dobson, Julian 25, 48, 76, 122
Dorney, Kate 4

eco-localism 14
economy, cultural 9
Edensor, Tim 69, 82
Edwards, Annie 78
Edwards, Gemma 4
Ellis, Hugh 121
England's Creative Coast 72
Eton College 22
exchange 119, 123
experiments 6–7, 8, 82, 85, 86–89

Fallows, Shaun 54, 59–60
Farnham, Surrey, UK 8
Farnham Maltings Theatre and Craft Studios, Surrey, UK 16–21

Fazackerley, Louise 2
Feher, Michel 48–49
Florida, Richard 4
Flynn, Molly 88
foodbanks 15, 17, 35
Forbes, Deborah 66
Fowler, Corinne 15
funding 5–7, 16, 26, 84, 108, 116, 117, 120
Future Arts Centres 8–9

Garden City 121, 122, 123
Garland, Jon 30
Gauntlett, David 13
gentrification 4, 71, 76
Gerrard, Dominique 83–86, 88
ghosts 119
gift economy 8
Good Chance Theatre 1; Little Amal 1, 7, 9
Gopinath, Gayatri, queer regional imaginary 43, 58–59
Gordon, Avery 97–98, 99, 103, 105, 106, 110–112
Gray, Cara 87
Greater Manchester, UK 1, 7, 93, 94, 99, 101, 104, 105, 112, 119; Mayor Andy Burnham 1
Green Party 28; Roberts, Sue 29
Greene, Anne-marie 32
Grice, Darren 120, 121
Guinan, Joe 124
Gunn, Susannah and Powe, Neil 30
Gurney, Peter 119

Hall, Catherine 44
Handspring Puppet Company 1
Hanson, Steve 124
Harlem Renaissance 41, 57–58
Harris, Jose, civil society 43, 46
Harvey, Dee 78, 79
Harvie, Jen 4
Hastings, Sussex, UK 8, 9, 66–89
Hastings Contemporary Art Gallery 70
Hayle, UK 69
Henderson, Kate 121
heritage, assets 36
heritage, Jamaican 30
heritage, local 16, 18, 26, 27

Hertfordshire, UK 117
High Wycombe, Buckinghamshire, UK 14, 19
Hills, June 81
Historic England (*and*: Heritage Action Zone, High Streets Heritage Action Zone) 69, 120
Historic England 6, 43–44
Hochschild, Arlie Russell 16
Holdsworth, Nadine 66
hope, hopefulness 1–3, 6, 7, 8, 9, 119, 124
Hopkins, Rob 14
Howard, Ebenezer 121, 122, 123
Hughes, Langston 57–58
Hybrid model of theatre (also: amateur/professional collaboration) 78–80, 82–89

Immersive theatre 93, 94, 108, 109, 111
Incredible Edible 122
industrial decline (post-industrial towns) 42, 43–44
industrial landscapes 105; post-industrial landscapes 106, 110
Industrial Revolution 105
inequality, inequalities 2, 48, 53
Ingold, Tim 12, 67, 85

Jennings, Will 5

Kealey, Patrick 83–85
Keeler, Julie 78
Kispert, Matthias 123
KIT Theatre 93, 97, 102, 104, 107, 108–112
Klinenberg, Eric 18–19
Knott, Stephen 87, 88
Knowles, Kieran 102–103; *Some People Feel the Rain* 102–103
Kropotkin, Peter 123

Landy, Charles 4
Latour, Bruno 7
Lee, Jennie 5–6
Lefebvre, Henri 67, 69
Leigh, Greater Manchester, UK 8, 9
Leigh Ladies Anti-Slavery Committee 106–107

Letchworth Arts and Leisure Group 117
Letchworth Garden City 117, 119, 121, 123
Letchworth Settlement 117, 122
levelling up 5, 45, 48; as political spectacle 48
Lewes, UK 123
Lindsay, Ripton 47
Linkon, Sherry 106
Little Theatre Guild, The 9, 26, 32, 66
Local Exchange Programme 93, 99–102, 109, 112
local government 5
local identities 16
local knowledge 12
local resilience 22
local stories 22–26
localism 8, 13–16, 18, 37–38
locality 14, 21–22, 37–38
Lock, Katy 121
Lowe, Lisa 44

MacFayden, Peter 21
Madanipour, Ali 14
Manners, David 79, 86
Margate, UK 71–72
McCann, Philip 5
McGrath, John 18
McKinnie, Michael 4
Medici effect 45, 48
memory 12, 13
Merkin, Ros 4
meshworks 67, 74, 85, 88, 120, 124
Milk Presents 25
Milling, Jane 66
Millington, Steve 69
Mouffe, Chantal 24
Mould, Oli 4, 74, 123
Moving Roots 42, 53–54, 56
mutual aid 6, 123, 124

Nandy, Lisa (Wigan MP) 3–4
National Theatre 32, Public Acts 1, 98–99
neoliberalism 4
networks 94, 95, 99, 101, 102, 103, 104, 105, 118, 120, 122, 124
New Municipalism 51–52

Index

Nicholson, Helen 88
Nicholson, Helen, Holdsworth, Nadine and Milling, Jane 66
Northern Powerhouse 49
Northern Soul 56, 59–60

Old Courts, The 42, 44, 50–51, 52, 56, 59, 61
Olusoga, David 105, 106, 107
O'Neill, Martin 124
Orwell, George 42, 49–50

partnership 8
Pearson, Mike 109; *Marking Time* 107–108
Potter, Katy 18
Pritchard, D 42, 53–54, 57, 60–61
Public Works, New York 98
Punter, Michael 83–86, 89

Reed, Jon 81
regeneration 8
rent parties 41–42, 56, 57–58, 60–61
Rent Party 41–42, 54–62
repertoire 8, 9
resilience 124
Rex, Bethany and Campbell, Peter 5
Rhythms, seasonal and daily 69, 81–83, 89
Richardson, Jane 79, 83
Ridgeway Community Church, Wallingford 25–36; Lloyd-Jones, Gareth; Whiting, Karen
Roach, Joseph 14
Robinson, Jo 4
Rochdale, UK 94, 100, 116, 117, 119, 120, 121, 123
Rochdale Pioneers 119, 123
Royal Court Theatre, The (Wigan) 44, 50–51
Royal Exchange Theatre (Manchester) 93–94, 103–104, 109, 111–112

Sanghera, Sathnam 15
Santos, Boaventura de Sous; abyssal lines 46, 47–48
Sellman, Neil 66, 67, 71, 75, 77, 79–82, 86–88
Shabazz, Lasana, *I am Wycombe* 19

Shah, Preena 71, 75
Shanks, Michael 109
Shine, Leigh 73
Shucksmith, Mark 15
site-specific theatre 94, 97, 109, 111
slavery, legacies of 46–47, 49–50
Slough, Berkshire, UK 8, 14, 16, 21, 22–26
Smith, Ali 20
social experiment(s) 118, 119, 123
social haunting 97, 99, 103–104, 106, 110–111
social services 15
Solnit, Rebecca 2, 3, 6, 9, 16, 119
South East England 14,16, 18, 22, 37
spectacle, political 5
Spinners Mill, Leigh 96, 102–104, 109, 111–112
Stables Theatre, Hastings 66–68, 73–74, 76–89
Steer, Mel 15
Stewart, Kathleen 103
Stewart, Susan 19
storytelling, 17, 19, 24
Stride, Gavin 17, 18, 21
Stroud, UK 122
structure of feeling 14, 21, 31
sustainability 7, 38; environmental 14, 28, 36

Tachauer, Janet 77
The Localism Act 2011 15
The Office for National Statistics 3
theatre building 8, 76–77
Theatres Trust 118
Todd, Liz 15
Todmorden, UK 122
Totnes, UK 122
town, towns, definition of 3; population of 3; towns and cities 5, 9
Town and Country Planning Association 121, 122
Town planning 119, 121
Transition Towns 14, 122
Tribe Arts 47, 62–63
Turnbull, Olivia 4

UK EU Referendum (Brexit) 5, 98, 99
Urquhart, Julie 72

Voluntary Community and Social Enterprise sector 75
Volunteer-led theatre 66–67, 77–81
Volunteers, Volunteering, 8, 9, 13, 15, 16, 23–24, 28, 34, 67, 74–81, 117, 119, 120

Wallingford, Oxfordshire, UK 8, 16, 26–36, 38; Bunkfest 28–29; Mayor Marcus Harris 28–30, 35
Walmsley, Ben 12–13
Warburton, John 31, 32, 33
Ward, Jonathan 71
White Rock Theatre, Hastings 72–73
Whitty, Chris 75
Whybrow, Nicolas 4
Wigan, cultural manifesto, *The Fire Within* 47, 51
Wigan, Greater Manchester, UK 1, 9
Wigan, King Street 43–44, 47; The Galleries 49
Wigan, *The Wigan Deal* 48, 51–52
Wigan, UK 94, 95, 97, 104
Wigan Youth Brass Band 1–2
WigLe Dance 1–2
Williams, Andrew, Goodwin, Mark, and Cloke, Paul 15
Williams, Eric 107
Williams, Raymond 14, 17, 35, 97, 104, 119; resources of hope 97, 104, 112
Windsor Theatre Royal 22
Woollaston, Jackie 78
working class artists 53–54, 55
Wright, Gloria 33–34

Zebracki, Martin 71